You OK, Christy?

ISBN: 978 1 89768552 5

Published 2018 in Ireland by Onstream,
Currabaha, Cloghroe, County Cork, Ireland.
www.onstream.ie

Book production: Nick Sanquest

Print: Fermoy Print & Design Ltd.

You OK, Christy?

MEMOIRS OF A SURVIVOR

Christy Fleming

'Mousie,' an orphan from Mwene Ditu who loved boxing, 1961

contents

In 1967, I worked for London Transport as a bus conductor on the number 73 route that went through the West End of London all the way to Richmond. On my day off, while out to the shops, I felt very tired and made my way to a café for a rest. A few minutes later I felt worse and left to get some fresh air. Soon after, I went into a grand mal epileptic seizure, and when I recovered from that, I went straight into another attack. When I finally woke, three policemen were holding me down, one with his knee on my chest, pinning my arms to the ground. The other two officers were holding my legs, which was painful. I panicked and tried to throw them off. To be honest, I have no idea where I found the strength. I then went into yet another attack, and the next thing I knew, I was in an ambulance, parked outside a mental hospital, with three police officers and a medic.

I went berserk, pushing them away from me. Then I again passed out.

When I came to, I was in a mental hospital cell, lying on a mattress on the ground with blood all over my face and clothes. I had no idea what I had done. They told me that I had attacked the police officers that were trying to help me, and, because they couldn't control me, had brought me to a mental hospital.

A memory came back to me of fighting off people who were holding me down. I could visualise, from when I was thirteen years old, a priest and two Rosminian Brothers restraining me while an old priest took photos and sexually abused me. However, I didn't remember actually fighting off the police officers. It appears that I had been having a flashback. But, because I had fought the three police officers, the health authorities regarded me as a violent person, so I was sectioned to remain in the mental hospital for assessment. This made me so angry. I knew I didn't have mental health problems. I was depressed and frustrated and was very aware of my condition, but was in total control of my depression. Sectioning me was so unnecessary, and very upsetting for me because of the way I was treated.

At no time did the doctors realise that I suffered from epileptic seizures. In fact, I wasn't completely sure myself that I had epilepsy, because at that point I had never heard of it. I just thought I was having blackouts. After a few days in the hospital, they diagnosed my condition because I had several seizures while there, brought on by the stress of being sectioned. I couldn't bear the thought of being controlled by all these people in white coats. I had spent too much of my childhood being controlled by men of the cloth in industrial schools.

I made an attempt to escape and ended up on the hospital roof. The police were called and I was very quickly caught and returned to my hospital cell. The local newspapers printed the story the following day:

'Man goes berserk on hospital rooftop'

I wasn't too sure if my flashbacks were as a result

of the sexual abuse forced on me in two different residential schools run by religious Brothers in Ireland, or if they were as a result of my experience serving with the United Nations in the Congo in 1961. The flashbacks seemed to have elements of both, and I never took much notice of them until I started to have seizures.

So, I have now decided to write about my journey of life once and for all, and, hopefully, kick out the demons inside my head. It wasn't all doom and gloom, there was also joy and humour. A story that needs to be told.

Christy and his twin sister, Margaret, c. 1946

To my loving wife, Mary (known to her family as Mai).

With thanks to my great friend, Muiris de Barra and his wife Esther for all their help with this book, and to Roz Crowley of Onstream Publications.

Christy at 17, two days before leaving for the Congo

one

EARLY DAYS

My twin sister Margaret and I were born on February 13, 1944. We lived in Markievicz House on Townsend Street, Dublin, with my widowed mother and two brothers. There were eight blocks, A to H; we lived in G Block. We were never well off, but we were not aware of it.

My dad died when I was 13 months old so I can't remember him. I do remember when I was about six or seven years of age telling my friends that my dad was in England working and that he wrote to me. That was one big fat lie, but it made me feel great because my friends were always talking about their dads. I have good memories of my childhood up to the age of twelve. Then I started to rebel against going to school.

I attended Westland Row Christian Brothers School and hated every day I spent there. My eyesight wasn't very good and I wasn't learning anything because I was always sitting at the back of the class and could never clearly see the blackboard. This resulted in me being held back for a year. The same thing happened the following year, leaving me in a class with children two years younger than me. By the time I was twelve, I refused to go to school. I didn't see any point because I knew it had given up on me.

I did many jobs, like selling papers on the corner at the Bank of Ireland, opposite Trinity College, Dublin. I worked for a newspaper seller who was nicknamed Jingles. It was a brilliant pitch and I was making enough money to take home. I worked part-time as a messenger boy, travelling on a bike all over Dublin City making deliveries for a dental clinic. I also earned some money collecting turf for my neighbours with a box cart I built using pram wheels. I charged sixpence for two sacks of turf and I was able to carry eight sacks at a time.

If there was a wedding or a party in the flats, the celebrations would move down to the square outside. There were eight rectangular blocks of flats with concrete walls around them. Part of the square had sheds for storing prams and bikes, and residents each had their own shed key. The large open part of the square is where we played football and where celebrations took place. Everyone would join in the music. I loved all that.

There was an old lady who lived on the ground floor and I would go to the shops for her. My mother had the key of her flat, and dropped in to check on her most days. One morning, my mother gave me the key to check if she wanted any shopping. I let myself in and found the lady apparently asleep on her bed. I didn't want to leave without checking if she needed anything, so I approached the bed and shook her gently. She didn't respond, and when I touched her hand I noticed how cold she was. I realised the poor lady was dead. With my heart pounding, I ran out of the flat to tell my mother. I was terrified. It was quite an experience for a nine-year-old boy and I remember it as clear as if it was yesterday.

The usual hangout on Townsend Street was to the rear of the shops on the ground floor of my block. In the forties and fifties, a lot of the lads would hang out there with Teddy Boys. On most days, with little else to do, it was the place to be. Sometimes they would club around to buy a football for one and sixpence and organise a match in the square. Other times, some of them would bring their guitars and play music and we'd all sing along.

There were times as a kid when my friends and I got up to mischief. I can recall when I was about eight years old and we found a way to make money in the city. We never stole or did anything that could be classed as illegal; we just used ingenuity to get small amounts of money from people.

We would make our way to a cinema on O'Connell Street where there would be a large queue. One of my friends would push me against the line of people and I would pretend to be thrown to the ground. Then my friends would 'attack' me, and I would scream and cry my eyes out as if I was being beaten. The people in the queue would rescue me by pulling my 'attackers' away and demand to know why they were beating me. The two of them would say that the reason they were angry with me was because I had lost our bus fare and all three of us would have to walk all the way out to Ballyfermot – quite a distance. It worked every time: they would put their hands in their pockets and give us enough money to pay our bus fares all the way out to the suburbs. It was clear profit, as all three of us lived just a short distance away.

We would then make our way to another cinema

and pull off the same scam. Each time we did it, we swapped the one to be pushed into the queue. Once we had enough money, we made our way to the hot-dog place in O'Connell Street and bought three.

On one particular day, we went into the city to do the usual thing. When we got to the queue, I was pushed to the ground as planned. But, when I landed I felt an terrible pain in my side. It was so bad I cried for real, but managed to pick myself up before the other boys started to 'attack' me. They couldn't understand what was going on because I walked away holding my side. I made my way home, to find that Mam was still at work. I really needed to see her because she would know what to do to help.

It got so bad that I decided to make my own way to Patrick Dun's hospital. I knew something bad was happening to me and I was very frightened. When I got to the casualty department, I collapsed onto the floor and was rushed into Intensive Care. I heard a doctor say that my mother needed to be contacted as quickly as possible. I was able to tell them that she worked in the government buildings on Merrion Street. They arranged for the police to find her and she was brought to the hospital in a squad car. My appendix had burst and they needed her to sign a consent form so that they could operate on me.

I was rushed into surgery, as a burst appendix is very dangerous. They put cotton wool over my face to put me to sleep. I panicked and pulled it off, spitting out pieces of cotton wool. The surgeon slapped me in the face and warned me not to be spitting at him; he wouldn't believe that I was spitting out pieces of cotton wool. He placed it back over my face, held it firmly against my nose and before I knew it, I was out for the count. I woke up in the men's ward, still in a lot of pain. I cried all night long.

There was an old man in the bed next to me and he gave me some jelly sweets. He was a lovely man and meant well, thinking the sweets would help me with my pain. I couldn't eat them, as I couldn't chew, so I tucked them under my pillow.

One of the patients called for a nurse to check on me. She looked at my stitches, only to find that they had broken and the wound was infected. So, back into surgery, I went through the same thing again with the cotton wool putting me to sleep. Only this time, I didn't really care what they did to me as long as they knocked me out. The pain was killing me. After a few days I was out of danger and my mam was told that she nearly lost me. When she told me this I felt so sad for her, I could see she was very emotional.

She told me that Dad died at the age of thirty-three from a burst appendix and that's why she got so upset. She said that he had complained of pains for several days but couldn't take time off work because he was on piecework, paid by the hour. That's how I discovered how he died. I was so angry with him because he should have done what I did and got to hospital in time.

After all the horrible pain I went through, I could only imagine what he had endured and I got emotional thinking about him. I was only nine years old and, finding out what happened to him, I felt life was unfair, really unfair.

Mam hugged me and told me about the time he saved all of our lives from a fire in our one-bedroom flat. My twin sister and I were in our cot in the living room, while my two brothers were asleep in the bedroom. It was a cold evening, and my dad was due home any minute, so she started to load turf onto the fire to warm the flat before he got home. She had a problem getting it started and decided to throw some paraffin onto it. The flames shot out onto the floor and over the armchairs. She screamed and tried to put it out with a jug of water. The fire was getting completely out of control and was spreading further. She tried to drag the cot towards the door. It was then that Dad arrived home and managed to get it under control, but there was already a lot of damage to the furniture. She told me that if he hadn't turned up when he did, there was a great possibility we would all have died in that flat.

He was a quiet man and never got angry with her for throwing the paraffin onto the fire, just told her not to worry. We were all safe and nothing else mattered.

My friends' and my scam at the cinemas ended when my older brother Jimmy found out what we were doing and told my mother, who in turn told the other boys' parents. We never did go back to our role-playing of fist-fighting again. I didn't speak to Jimmy for a week after that. He referred to us as The Little Mafia, but to be fair, he always looked out for me. He was very protective, a big brother I looked up to.

Life in Dublin in the forties and fifties was full of hardship for my mam. She worked two shifts a day, one in the early hours of the morning and then an evening shift, five days a week, and one early shift on Saturday. Even at my age, I worried about how hard she worked and I would try to help out by washing the floors at home before she came home from work. She used to have a great laugh when she would walk in and see all the newspapers scattered across the floor.

I used the newspapers to dry it off.

My aunt Maggie, Dad's sister, would come every morning to wake the four of us up and get us off to school. Breakfast was tea and toast, which was toasted on the gas cooker. When we got home from school in the afternoon, Mam would have cooked for us before her evening shift, and then Aunt Maggie would collect us from the play area of the flats and get us ready for bed.

Markievicz House, 1950s, Dublin

PE class in Greenmount School playground

Greenmount School dormitory

two

AN EDUCATION

My mam worked very hard bringing up four of us on her own, and it didn't get any easier when she found out I wasn't attending school. She did her very best to persuade me to go, but I refused. I continued to do odd jobs around Dublin earning a few shillings. I knew it was only a matter of time when I would get caught and be in trouble with the school authorities.

Eventually, I did get caught and Mam had to appear with me in court. They informed her that I was to be sent to a residential industrial institution until the age of sixteen. They said that because I refused to go to school I was uncontrollable, and denied her request to send me to a local one where she might have be able to visit me. The court issued an order that I be sent to Greenmount Industrial School in Cork City. My mam wasn't allowed to see me before I was taken away by the court. That was difficult.

When I was about ten years old, I remember seeing a movie starring Jeff Chandler. He played a big-time lawyer who sent his young son to a residential college. The son was shown around the college and when he was shown his room he got all excited. It was quite large and it was lined with full bookshelves.

Stupidly, I thought maybe I would be given my own

room with lots of books and that I would be educated, because learning is what I always wanted. I often watched Mam sitting by the fire reading her newspaper and I used to wish I could do the same. I wasn't too upset about being sent away to a residential industrial school, thinking some good may come of it.

That was very far from the truth.

I was taken from Dublin by rail, escorted by a plainclothes policeman, and dropped off at the school around 8pm on a Wednesday.

The Presentation Brothers and several tradesmen in Cork City ran Greenmount Industrial School. (I have to refrain from using the real names of the Presentation Brothers in Greenmount School for legal reasons, so I will use made-up forenames.)

The head Brother, John, a tall, slim built, bald headed man, dressed in a black habit and white neck-collar, greeted us. He escorted me to the sleeping quarters, what we called the dormitory. There were two of them. I was taken to one on the first floor. There were six lines of beds the whole length of it, and I was given the first vacant bed in the first line and instructed to undress and put on a long nightshirt. So much for the room with lots of bookshelves. I remember feeling scared and very unhappy and kept wishing I was home with my mam and family. But I knew it was entirely my own fault.

I was twelve years and three months old, and I would have to spend the next three years and nine months in this institution where some boys were sent for stealing, some because they had no parents, and others there for the same reason as me.

That first night was the longest of my life. A night watchman kept marching into the dormitory every couple of hours pulling each kid out of their bed to make them go to the toilet. He started with the first line, which I learned later was the line for the 'wet the beds'. I wasn't too happy being woken every two hours and made to go to the toilet, although I was not getting much sleep anyway.

At seven the next morning, the watchman made his final visit to see that we were all up and dressed. He then checked each mattress. Any one he found wet, that boy would have to half turn their mattress onto the back of his bed. This meant that Brother John could see what boys had wet their bed and take their names.

When I got back from the toilet, the Brother was standing by my bed, asking me why I didn't turn over my mattress. I knew that I had not wet the bed and told him, "Because I have never wet my bed." Suddenly, out of the blue, he slapped me across the face, knocking me to the floor. I picked myself up and I figured out that one of the regular 'wet the beds' swapped his wet mattress onto my bed while I was in the washroom. The Brother proceeded to call out a list of names of those who had wet their beds and we were instructed to wait outside the office.

I suddenly realised that no matter what I said, I would not be believed, and that punishment would be handed out whether I was innocent or guilty. This was only the beginning.

After breakfast, one of the boys told me that we would be punished for wetting our beds and this was the routine each morning. He also told me that swapping mattresses with new boys was common practice.

The Brothers and staff were not the only ones who handed out corporal punishment. Older boys who were called Prefects were just as bad. They loved picking on the younger boys, bullying and beating them for no good reason, just to show who was in charge. Some of these Prefects were also responsible for sexually abusing the younger boys. These same Prefects were in turn abused by some of the Brothers.

It was hard to get used to the system of the school, and I found that keeping a low profile was my best chance of survival. I shared a table with several other boys at breakfast in a large dining room. We had porridge with salt, not sugar. Sugar was the privilege of the men of the cloth only. Then we had two slices of bread and dripping with tea.

I still hadn't got over the shock of the slap that floored me on that first day, and the thought of being punished for something I didn't do made me really anxious. I was scared, and had to fight hard to hold back the tears. After breakfast, we were taken into the office to Brother John, and each one of us got six slaps of the leather on each hand. These leather straps were embedded with coins and they really hurt.

I remember thinking that if I knew which one of those boys swapped my mattress, I would challenge him, but that wasn't going to happen, and just as well, because I would have suffered a much worse punishment if I was caught fighting.

Instead of putting me into a class to learn, I was put into the kitchen to work. So much for the Court sending me here to get an education. I wasn't very popular with the other boys for getting this job. They would do anything to work there because there was always plenty of food for the kitchen workers.

The whole thing was a nightmare. I kept thinking, "How I am going to cope with this horror for the next three and a half years?" Little did I know things were going to get worse. Other lads told me I had to learn to stand up for myself or spend my time being bullied by the older boys. It seems all new boys were picked on and bullied and had to get wise and fight back, or spend every minute of every day being bullied until they reached the age of the sixteen and could leave.

After a couple of days in the school, I asked Brother John if I could write home to Mam. He roughly grabbed my arm and shouted into my ear, "You only arrived here two days ago and are already demanding things." He clipped my ear and threw me like a rag doll to the ground.

As the days passed, I quickly learned who and who not to be involved with, and that I had to watch my back at all times. But I also knew in my heart that it was impossible to survive here on my own. I had to find a friend I could trust.

three

PUNISHMENT

On my second week, I was sitting at the table with four nervous looking younger boys and a fifth older boy who was bigger than me. He was the Table Prefect.

He would bully us, and take from each of the younger boys what we called a 'square bashan', which was a slice of bread and dripping. He demanded respect from us as if he was one of the staff. He was one big shit of a bully and I hated the sight of him. The trouble started when he ordered me to hand over my slice of bread and dripping and to pour out his tea. I was advised by the younger boys not to tangle with this fifteen-year-old dictator. I handed him my bread and poured out his mug of tea. Without any warning, he proceeded to pour the hot tea over me. This was his way of teaching me never to hesitate when he gave me an instruction.

I completely lost it. I grabbed my own mug of tea and emptied it into his face and rugby-tackled him, grabbing his body and forcing him to the ground. I had to rugby tackle him because of his age and height. I knew if I did nothing, he would come after me at another time when I least expected it, so I kept punching him until one of the Brothers pulled me off him. This Brother brought me to the office and told me to sit and wait for Brother John to deal with me. Fighting in the school was taken seriously and the punishment was severe. I remembered that was the first piece of advice I was given on my first day.

I heard Brother John's footsteps approacing along the long corridor where I was sitting and he passed me and entered his office, saying nothing. About twenty minutes later he came out, checked that I was still there and went back inside. This continued for two hours. He knew I was terrified. This was part of the punishment. Eventually he called me in and told me to stand by his desk as he locked the door.

He moved over to the side of his desk, still saying nothing. I watched him as he proceeded to carefully remove his dark jacket, then his white collar. He paused for several seconds and rolled up his shirtsleeves very slowly, generating more dread. As I watched, I wet myself. He wasn't too pleased when he saw his wet office floor.

In a sharp, angry, loud voice, he instructed me to place my hand flat on his old, heavy, dark wooden desk. I put down my hand, palm facing upwards, thinking I just wanted to get this over with quickly. He reached for a bamboo cane and began swinging it firmly up and down. I could hear the whooshing sound as he swung it close to me. He told me to turn my hand with the palm facing down and to remain still. This was the last thing I expected. My whole body shook. He whacked the back of my hand as hard as he could six times and then made me put my other hand on the desk. He continued with a similar whacking on this hand. I fought back my tears, and he got even angrier because I didn't cry.

He repeated the beating, and this time I cried out for him to stop. The backs of both my hands were turning blue and starting to swell. The skin was broken. When he saw this, he shouted at me to hold out the palms of my hands and started to hit me so hard that I shrank back and then slipped on the wet floor. This made him even angrier and he started to hit me all over my body as I lay there. I could see his face and neck getting redder and redder with the effort, the sweat pouring down. He was completely out of control, and my screaming made him worse. I find it hard to describe those two hours, but it was obvious to me that this monster of a man took pleasure in inflicting pain.

Another Brother who was passing the office heard me screaming. He shouted through the door at Brother John, demanding that he unlock the door. Brother John was now beating me across my legs and back. I somehow managed to get on to my feet, ran to the door, unlocked it and collapsed. The other Brother ran in and managed to stop Brother John hitting me any further.

This other Brother saw the condition of my wounds and brought me to the nurse for treatment. She bandaged my hands and legs where the skin had broken. This severe, merciless beating had me in pain for weeks before my body started to heal. My mind took an awful lot longer.

I remember thinking, this is going to go on until my release date at the age of sixteen, and it terrified me to think that date was so far away.

I was moved from working in the kitchen, which I enjoyed, to working outside farming and digging potatoes in the plot at the back of the school. This seemed like further punishment.

I made one very good friend. His name was Ginger. He was a Cork lad who had been sent to the school at the age of six. Like me, Ginger hated the place. But, he had already spent six years there and knew the ropes. I was lucky to have a friend with so much experience.

I must have been there for five or six months when Ginger told me that he knew a way to get out of the building without being noticed, and asked me to join him in an escape. I didn't hesitate for one moment because it was something that was on my mind from the day I arrived. It would give me the opportunity to go to Dublin to see my family that I missed very much. I never had any visits from Mam. She couldn't afford to travel and stay over in Cork, as well as having three other kids to look after. The thought of running away scared me because I knew that, if we were caught, the punishment would be very severe and would be followed by a head shave. I had already seen one boy in the yard with his head completely shaved.

Our plan was simple. We waited until dark for the night watchman to finish his first patrol of the dormitory. Knowing his next inspection wouldn't be for another two hours, we knew that we would have at least that amount of time to get as far away from the school as possible. We borrowed pillows from some of the other boys to replace our bodies in the empty beds. We would have a headstart of a few hours before our absence would be noticed.

The day of the escape finally came, and it was around 2am when we sneaked down the stairs and made our way to the kitchen, where the back door opened out on to a field. Ginger had a pillowslip full of apples that we stole from the kitchen.

The darkness was scary and, being so close to the city, we realised that we couldn't just walk around Cork in the middle of the night because we could be noticed and picked up very quickly. We decided to lie low for a couple of hours until it got light, so we spent the rest of the night sheltering in a seating area in a park. We slept right through until about 8.30am when we were woken by the noise of a grass cutter in the distance.

We walked out onto the streets of Cork but had no clue which way to go. Ginger noticed a bike up against a railing, grabbed it and ran away with it as fast as he could. When I caught up with him, he said he had never ridden a bike and that I would have to ride it with him on the handlebars. It was a girl's bike with no crossbar!

We cycled around aimlessly and ended up in an area called Spangle Hill. A Garda on a bike spotted us and shouted at us to stop. Once I saw it was a Garda, I pedalled faster down the hill. The bike was difficult to control, with Ginger trying to balance on the handlebars. The Garda had almost caught up with us and shouted at us to stop, but I just kept pedalling like a madman down this endless hill. He passed us out and suddenly braked in front of us, forcing us to stop. When I squeezed the brakes to avoid hitting him, they failed to work and we collided. The three of us were stretched out in the middle of the road covered in cuts and scrapes, with the stolen apples scattered all over the road.

I managed to scramble to my feet and tried to run for it, but I could hear the Garda shouting, "Stop, or I'll kick the arse off you, boy." I stopped and he caught me by the collar and dragged me to where Ginger was sitting on a wall inspecting his wounds. We both ended up in the Garda station and Brother John was informed where we were and to come and collect us. The police were very kind to us. They gave us a warm mug of tea and as many buns as we wanted. We were picked up and taken back to the institution in a white van. We never spoke during the journey.

Ginger and I were severely beaten with the leather strap and we had a path worn to the nurse's surgery for many days while she treated our wounds. Why did she not report these attacks to a higher authority?

Corporal punishment was a common practice in these institutions, despite the rules to the contrary. Children who ran away were subjected to extreme physical punishment. Not being content with just dishing out pain as expected, to further humiliate us, Brother John shaved our heads in front of all the other boys.

I had never had my head shaved before and I was in tears. In some ways, all the children in the school were punished when a child ran away. They would take away any privileges such as the occasional movie or walk, which meant Ginger and I were then a target of resentment by other children and staff. I can remember thinking how good it had felt being free from that institution for twelve hours. It made me think hard about escaping again. But, the next time it would be with a better plan that would enable me to get to Dublin.

four

UPTON

Ginger and I were monitored closely for about three months. Each night one of the Brothers stood over us while we undressed and got into our nightshirts, and our clothes and shoes were taken out of the dormitory to ensure we couldn't run away. We were called 'runners', and we were not the only ones. The staff were very much aware of all of us, as our shaved heads were a giveaway.

This type of monitoring started to ease off in the third month, and eventually stopped. For a couple of weeks, we kept out of trouble, until I was caught smoking in the toilets by Brother Dan. He was a tall well-built man in his thirties. He interrogated me, demanding to know where I got the cigarette. He kept slapping me across the face until I gave him an answer. I could feel both sides of my cheeks burning from the constant slaps. I told him I found it in the yard, but he wasn't having any of it. He proceeded to grab both my ears tightly and lifted me off the ground as high as he could and then threw me to the ground. Jesus, the pain was so bad and my ears were hot and painful. He realised he had gone too far when I fell over as I tried to get to my feet. He eventually walked away, giving me a warning about smoking.

That incident certainly influenced my thinking about another escape from this hellhole, to get away from these sadistic animals.

There were two black boys among us in the school. We called them Small Darkie and Big Darkie, which was not considered offensive in the fifties. They were very popular among the boys and they seemed to have no objection to these nicknames.

Ginger was very close to Small Darkie, and all three of us got talking about another escape. Over several days we made a plan, again aiming to run at night because we would be too conspicuous during the day.

Small Darkie slept in the dormitory above Ginger and me, so we agreed to stay awake so that Ginger could sneak up to Darkie's dormitory around 2am to wake him. The three of us would head for the kitchen to make our escape. The plan, we thought, was perfect and we waited until the following night to proceed.

But Ginger didn't stay awake, and I didn't wake up as planned either. But Darkie did and, when he realised we must still be asleep, he got dressed and sneaked down to our dormitory to wake us. It was very dark, and he had to find his way to my bed, which was next to Ginger's. When he got to my bed, he shook me gently and whispered in my ear to get dressed. I was in a really deep sleep and as I opened my eyes all I could see was a black face looking down at me. I roared my head off, waking up the whole dormitory. Darkie jumped back, also screaming with fright and then most of the boys started screaming too. Some of the younger ones ran out of the dormitory crying and shouting that they were been attacked. Pandemonium!

Amidst all the commotion, I realised it was only Darkie, but it was too late, and he had to run back to his own dormitory and get undressed before the night watchman noticed his absence.

One of the Brothers came rushing into the dormitory in a dressing gown, demanding to know who did all the screaming. It didn't take long for one of the prefects to point to my bed. I explained to the Brother that I had a very bad nightmare and that I was very sorry.

Darkie wouldn't speak to me for weeks. He was angry, and rightly so. So much for the great escape that didn't happen, but when we got over the frustration and were speaking again, we decided that we should have another go.

One day we were all called to Assembly and told that Greenmount School was to close down the next day. We would be sent to other schools by bus the following morning. They split us into two groups and informed us which school we were being sent to. Ginger, Darkie, and I were part of the group going to Upton Industrial School in County Cork. I was very disappointed I wasn't going with the other group who were being sent to Artane, in Dublin. Up there my mam could visit me, which meant I would not get as much abuse as boys who never had visits.

I was then thirteen years and three months old.

The Rosminian Order of the Holy Brothers ran Upton Industrial School. Located in an isolated place out in the countryside, the nearest town, Bandon, was about five miles away. We were taken there by bus and the journey was endured in silence. It was a most depressing journey for all of us, with everyone either staring out the window or down into their lap. Brother Peter, the head Brother met us and took us to our accommodation. It looked and felt the same as the dormitories at Greenmount.

I had thought Greenmount was a right shithole and it clearly was, but Upton made it seem luxurious, and that's not exaggerating.

I was put to work in the boiler room with another boy a year older than me. We had to keep the steam pressure up in a huge boiler which provided the heating for the school and the kitchen. It was at the back of the school and it looked out on to the farms where Ginger and Darkie were put to work with other boys. The farm was about two hundred and fifty acres.

Fuel for the boiler was strips of leather and used lorry and bus tyres. The metal rings had to be cut out of these, and the rubber chopped into short pieces to be fed into the furnace. It was a man's job, not a boy's one, but I had to learn very quickly how to cope. It was very hard work from 5.30am until 8pm, seven days a week. By the time I finished my day's work it was straight to my dormitory to bed.

Sometimes we had to work up to 10pm if we had trouble banking down the boiler. It was on one of those late nights, as I made my way to my dormitory, exhausted, that I saw Brother Peter standing outside his bedroom door in his dressing gown. His room was situated at the upper end of the dormitory.

He beckoned me into his room, saying that he wanted to talk to me. He wanted to know why I wasn't having any visits, and if I was upset about it. The conversation continued for about fifteen minutes after which he put his arm around me. He said that he and the staff in the school were now my family, insinuating that I should embrace it and get to like him. He took my hand and pushed it inside his dressing gown – he was naked underneath it – forcing it on to his penis. When I tried to squirm away, he pulled me back and attempted to pull my pants down. I held onto them, got myself free, and ran out of the room, shaking. I didn't know where I could hide. He followed me and told me to go to my bed and say nothing.

Brother Peter and Brother Aaron were two Brothers who were well known to be perverts. Brother Aaron had a habit of walking up and down the dormitory during the night and selecting a boy to abuse. He would pace slowly in his bare feet, wearing his black habit. In the quietness of the night the sound of the habit, rustling as he walked along the dark dormitory, was scary. We never knew which bed he would stop at.

One night, I was very late getting to bed and all the other boys were sleeping. The lights were already off and you could hear a pin drop. I got into my nightshirt and couldn't wait to get my head down on the pillow. I was tired and ached all over from slicing those tyres. My hands were sore and covered in painful cuts.

I was barely asleep when I was woken by the sound of sobbing. I sat up and could see the boy in the bed in front of me was sobbing under his blanket. I asked him if he was feeling sick. At first, he wouldn't talk to me so I sat on the end of his bed, desperately urging him to keep down the sound of his crying. He confided in me telling me he was in pain and struggled to tell me that his bum felt like it was burning. I immediately knew what had happened to him. I helped him out of the bed and brought him into the washroom where I filled a sink with lukewarm water. I asked him to pull up his nightshirt and sat him on the sink so that the water could soothe his pain. He told me it was helping. At no time did I ask him why his bottom was so sore.

This was when I realised that the abuse in this school was far worse than I had thought. It took me days to get over what that boy had been through. He was only about nine or ten but looked younger.

After this incident I knew that an escape had to take priority. I wouldn't let Darkie and Ginger down again. I was scared of the staff and the bullyboys, but I realised I had to toughen up, stand up for myself and get out of this place.

Mealtimes were the only opportunity I got to see Ginger and Darkie, and over the weeks we made our new escape plan. It was said by many of the boys that nobody ever broke out of Upton school without getting caught or returning back to the school voluntarily. It was rumoured that any boy who did a runner always ended up handing themselves up because they couldn't handle the hardship of the countryside. We knew that if we got caught, the punishment would land all three of us in the infirmary for days, if not weeks. But the risk was worth it. Anyone would think that we would have learned a lesson about running, but here we were again, planning.

Having been here for a while, we realised that the staff were confident that there would be no attempts at escaping, due to the fear of punishment, along with the fear of being stranded out in such wild countryside. Because of their overconfidence, getting out of this place would be easy. We hoped.

Ginger said he would go to England so they couldn't

track him down. Darkie wanted to go to the North of Ireland because somebody told him he had a brother living there and he wanted to find him. As for me, I just wanted to go home. I hadn't thought beyond that.

The other boy who worked in the boiler room was happy to cover for me while I met up with Darkie and Ginger to put our plan into operation.

This was it! We had only one chance and if we were caught, we would never get another opportunity to escape from this nightmare.

I arranged to meet them in the afternoon, on the farm where they were working. It was easy for me, as the boiler room was next to it. We slipped away unnoticed into the adjacent farmland. There were so many boys working in the fields that we would not be noticed. We knew that we wouldn't be missed until bedtime. We crossed a ditch, and took off as quickly as we could, making sure to stay out of sight, ducking below the top of the fence. Our hearts were pounding and we didn't really know where we were heading.

We struggled to find our way through the countryside and, after a couple of hours, Darkie fell into a ditch and hurt his ankle. He started limping, which didn't suit Ginger, who never stopped moaning that he was slowing us down.

Between Ginger moaning, Darkie limping, and the fear of being caught, tension was mounting between us. After a couple of hours walking, we spotted an old barn. Darkie wanted to hide in it for a couple of hours, hoping a rest would help his painful ankle. We agreed to rest there for a while.

Even though I wouldn't admit it, I also needed to rest. I realised how tired and undernourished I was after working so hard and from barely having had enough to eat over the past months.

We settled down in the barn and I closed my eyes and began to drift off to sleep. Suddenly Darkie was shouting his head off that the place was full of scampering rats. Stumbling and screaming, we got out of there in double quick time and carried on through the countryside, Darkie forgetting about his sore ankle.

We stayed off the roads by walking in the ditches. At around 8.30pm, it started to get dark and we moved back on to the road so that we could see where we were going. It was much safer out there than tripping over branches and stones inside the ditches. We had now been on the run for over ten hours and had so far managed to avoid being spotted by anyone. We saw car headlights approaching from the distance, and jumped back into the ditch and hid there until it passed. After another couple of hours, we were feeling very tired and decided to find a place to settle down for the night. We got as comfortable as we could in a ditch, but I think we might have had only two hours sleep at the most because we were so cold and, on top of that, Darkie was again whinging about the pain in his ankle.

Our objective was to get to Cork City, But Darkie said that he could never walk that far because of the pain in his ankle. He wanted to go to a hospital to be treated because he thought that it was broken. He became so desperate that he decided he would ask any passers-by on the road where the nearest hospital was located, or even try to hitch a lift.

It was now about 11am, and Darkie stuck out his

thumb for a lift. A lorry pulled over. Darkie asked where he was heading and the driver told him that he was on his way to Cork City. He told the driver how he had lost his bus fare back to Cork, and lied that he was staying at the Greenmount school. He hoped the man wasn't aware the school was closed down. "Hop in, laddie," invited the driver. Darkie pointed to us, and told him we were also heading back, so the three of us a got a lift all the way.

During the entire journey, the driver never stopped chatting. I was so tired that I fell asleep and woke up in a place called Ballyphehane, where he dropped us off. As we were leaving, he gave us some loose change to get the bus from there to Greenmount. This was the first act of kindness shown to us in a very long time. We thanked him and said our goodbyes. We had reached our first destination.

It had been so long since we had anything to eat, the first thing we needed to do was find a shop. Thankful for the money the driver had given to us, we bought a loaf of bread and some sweets. Darkie's priority was to get to a hospital. His ankle was much worse and he insisted that we split up and go our separate ways, knowing that if he stayed with us we could easily be recognised, him being a black boy. It made sense, so we agreed that, once we got him to the hospital, we would split up. By now his ankle was blue and swollen. Darkie asked a lady where the nearest hospital was, and we only had to walk a couple of minutes to get there. We were so relieved when a nurse took him in to a waiting room. Once we knew he was being looked after, Ginger and I agreed to go our separate ways too. We knew that was safer than staying together.

Upton Industrial School, Co. Cork

five

ON THE RUN

Now I was on my own I needed to decide what to do. I walked as fast as I could along the streets until I came to a bridge. There were rail tracks running down the middle of it. I made my mind up to follow them, thinking I might be able to sneak onto a train. When I got around the corner and looked to my right I realised that this was the very station I arrived at in Cork when I had been sent down from Dublin. It felt like a lifetime had passed.

I could feel my heart pounding in my chest, terrified that a Garda could be waiting around the next corner to catch me. I started to run away from the station, and only stopped when I knew that I was well away from it.

My original plan had been to hitch a lift and I now felt that perhaps this was the best option. By now I was completely lost, but kept walking anyway as I wanted to get on to a road going out of the city. After what felt like miles, I could see fields and ditches. Then, to my right I heard a train, and I could see it passing over a bridge. This made my mind up for me and I knew that following the tracks would be the quickest and surest way of getting home without getting caught and being sent back to that hellhole and those monsters.

I changed direction, and headed for the bridge. I couldn't risk jumping on to a train, so walking along the tracks would ensure that I was going the right way, and maybe I could even find a way of sneaking into a carriage at a station. But I really didn't care how long it took me to get to Dublin as long as I got there.

It wasn't too difficult to find my way to the rail tracks. About half a mile from the railway bridge, I found a path going up an embankment. I climbed over a fence, found myself at the tracks and started walking. I stayed close to the side so as not to be spotted. I walked for hours, ducking into the side-ditch if I heard a train coming. Several trains passed and I longed to be a passenger on one of them. I was covered in cuts and bruises from all the briars, as sometimes I had to crawl through them. I rested for an hour or so whenever I needed to, and continued walking, keeping my eyes on the tracks. They were the path to Dublin, and to freedom.

It was getting dark when I approached a very high railway bridge across a wide, fast-flowing river. The thought of having to cross it frightened me. I was not sure what to do next, so I hid in some bushes to rest and plan my next move. By now I was hungry and tired, so I finished off my bread and some of the sweets and drifted off to sleep.

I don't know how long I slept, but the sound of an oncoming train woke me with a start. As it passed, and I watched the lights disappear away from me over the bridge, I knew that I had to get across before another train came.

Running between the tracks as fast as I could without looking down at the dark river below, my heart pounded with fear. As I had almost reached the other side, my foot slipped, and I fell hard onto a wooden sleeper. As I lay there trying to get my breath back, I felt the rail vibrate, and thought there was another train coming. But, when I looked up, I could see that the vibration was from the one I had just followed, and that it seemed to be moving more slowly now. There must be a station just ahead. Feeling tired, sore, cold and hungry, I hoped that I could find somewhere there where I could finally get some decent rest.

As I cautiously approached the station, I noticed some apparently empty carriages on a siding. I moved towards them very carefully, tried all the doors, and found one that was unlocked. At last something was going my way.

I lay down on a long seat and immediately fell asleep. I don't know how long I slept, but I woke up shivering with cold. My whole body seemed to go into convulsions and I couldn't stop myself from shaking. I started to jump up and down swinging my arms, anything to get some warmth back into my body.

It was still dark but I felt that I might as well be walking as to stay here in the cold. I jumped out of the carriage and edged up on to the platform. The lights were on but I couldn't see anyone as I crept around. The sign on the platform said Mallow, and I remember some of the boys in Greenmount School talking about it. I knew this was a station on the Dublin line. I was going the right way. Hearing a noise, I hopped back down on the tracks and ran out of sight. I heard a door slamming and a voice call out but I didn't stop to find out who it was.

I got a surge of hopeful energy and headed off

quickly along the tracks. I walked for hours and felt the best I had in days, but hunger pangs eventually caught up with me, and my energy just drained away.

I sat down on the bank, took out the last of my sweets and and slowly sucked on one of them, trying to make it last as long as I could, because this was the last of my food. I was feeling quite relaxed, and drifted into a funny sort of sleep where I wasn't sure if I was dreaming or if it was real. So many thoughts kept flying in and out of my mind. The sound of a train brought me back to reality.

Dawn had broken. I resumed my journey, the tracks stretching out in front of me for as far as the eye could see. By now I had worked out how I could tell when a train was coming just by touching the rail with my hand or foot. That would give me time to merge into the ditches and hide.

There were some small stations along the way and I went through the fields to skirt them. While I was crossing one of these fields, I found some turnips in a feeder. Picking one up, I ran to the nearest ditch and looked for a sharp stone. My hands and fingers were numb from the cold and I cut my hands as I tried to peel it. Giving up on that, I just bit chunks off and ate my fill.

I broke up the remainder of the turnip, stuffed it in my pockets and headed out on the tracks again. Hours passed and darkness fell once more. Then, up ahead, I could see lights and knew that it was a major station. I moved into a field overlooking it and could see that it was called Limerick Junction. Below me I saw some sheds. Maybe I could get into one of them for the night. I waited for a train to pass and once the platform was empty I jumped over the ditch, headed to the sheds and found one open. In a corner I could see some cloth bags. I lay on the ground and wrapped them around me, ate a piece of turnip and closed my eyes.

Once more I woke early, but this time at least, I wasn't as cold. I ate a few more pieces of the turnip and gingerly crept out of the shed.

I had a quick look at the station clock on the platform. It was 5.20am, and this meant that I had a couple of hours before any trains would pass. Then I heard someone coming. I spotted a large clump of high grass and jumped into it. Instead of feeling the hard ground under me, I was falling down some sort of a hole. I hit the bottom fairly hard and the wind was knocked out of me. While I lay there, all my doubts and fears came rushing back – would I ever make it? What had I done to deserve all of this? My only crime was to stop going to school. Was anyone on my side?

I'm not sure how long I stayed down there feeling sorry for myself. I took another bite of turnip and pulled myself back towards the tracks, heading off once more.

There seemed to be a lot more trains passing this morning, and they were slowing me down as I had to hide every time. I decided to try going along the ditch and fields once again. This frustrated me as there were a lot of briars, barbed wire and thick grass to negotiate, which slowed me down even more.

I decided that it was too risky to walk during the day, so I settled down and slept in a safe spot behind some bushes. My plan now was to walk at night and sleep during the day to avoid the trains and being seen. The fact that the moon was out each night would make walking on the tracks a bit easier as I could see it reflecting on the rails. I guessed that it was about mid-afternoon now and, if I could fall asleep for a few hours, I could walk right through the night.

I woke up to loud shouting. I peeped out through the hedge and saw a farmer hunting his cattle back into the adjacent field. I waited until he disappeared and went around the field looking for another feeder and hopefully a turnip as I only had a little piece left in my pocket. No luck, but I did find a tap for water in a butt of sorts, and I gulped as much of it as I could and started walking again. When it got dark, I went back onto the tracks. Unfortunately, no moon appeared.

It was treacherous and scary in the blackness as I kept tripping over the rails and falling onto my knees, hurting them each time. Everything was so dark. I felt claustrophobic at times as the night seemed to engulf me.

I wondered how Ginger was getting on and if Darkie managed to sort out his ankle. I was feeling lonely and wished that we hadn't split up. This was surely my lowest point.

Despite walking most of the night, I seemed to be making little progress. I kept reminding myself that it didn't matter how long it took, as long as I got to Dublin. But I was too tired and weary to go any further so I hopped over the ditch and found a corner of the field with some cover and settled down to get some rest.

I could feel the wind blowing much stronger and colder. It was going right through me. I tried to worm myself further into the ditch to get more protection and fell into a fitful sleep.

It felt like only five minutes had passed when I woke up with water running down my face. As I heard the drops falling on the leaves of the bush, I realised that it had started to rain. At this stage it was pouring down and I was getting wet all over. I had to find a drier place, but where? I couldn't see any sign of a light or a building anywhere. I got up and started walking. After crossing another open field, I saw the outline of a big tree and headed towards it. The wind and rain were blowing into the large trunk as I put my back against it to shelter as best I could.

My thoughts turned to the loving, warm home waiting for me. Yet again, the thoughts became negative, doubting everything I had done. Why did I run away? Would I have been better off back there? I called for help from any good God out there. I was so low, my heart felt like breaking. How I missed the wit of Ginger and the strength of Darkie. If only they were here with me. We were such a strong team together.

Then all the horrible memories of what had happened back in those schools came flooding back and I knew that I was right to run and that I had the strength to make it. I had to persevere.

The rain eased off a little, so I decided to go on. I knew there wouldn't be any sleep today. Making my way back to the tracks, those bad memories seemed to give me the strength to push myself harder and faster. Whenever I needed to rest, I would go under a road bridge that crossed over the rail line, hiding behind a pillar, opposite to the direction of the oncoming trains.

This worked well and I avoided the heaviest of the rain by doing that. But I was soaked right through, and my whole body at this stage felt like it was covered in ice. It was getting dark again, and I knew I wouldn't last another night out in the cold. I had to find somewhere warm.

I had spent two nights in comfort of sorts in the two stations earlier on my route, and I made my mind up to check out the next station I came to. Being on the run now for three days and nights, I had to acknowledge my need for shelter and rest.

The next station I reached was a fairly large one called Portlaoise. I resolved that I had to somehow sneak onto a train. I came down the embankment just outside the station, slipping on the wet grass to the bottom. As I crept along the platform, I almost got caught when one of the staff called out, "Hey you, where do you think you're going?" I ran for my life out onto the streets of Portlaoise.

Hiding in a doorway, I got the smell of food. There was a café near the station so I hung around looking hungrily through the window and a waitress spotted me and called me inside. The first thing she said to me was, "My God, young man. Your face is filthy, what have you been doing, you poor thing?" Hearing an adult being so kind made me cry and this embarrassed me. I told the woman that I had walked from Cork City and was making my way to my home in Dublin. I had lost my rail ticket and the man in the Cork station hadn't believed me.

She took me to the back of the kitchen and wiped away the dirt off my face and washed my hands. She sat me down to a big fry-up. I couldn't believe my luck. I wolfed it down quickly and, seeing how starved I was, she put more fried eggs on my plate.

She was so angry with what I had told her about the man in the Cork station and said that she would complain about him. While I was eating, she went back into the café area telling the customers what had happened. She took up a collection from them so that I could buy a train ticket to Dublin. One of them walked me to the ticket office, bought my ticket and put me on the train. At no time did that woman or any of the customers question me as to why I was alone, and I often wondered if they realised that I was running from an industrial school, trying to get home to my family. I will never know, but I was so grateful to them for being so kind.

The train journey was uneventful, and I felt happy getting off at Kingsbridge Station (renamed Heuston in 1966) because I knew my way from there to Townsend Street and was very comfortable about walking home. I remember thinking that I never wanted to see railway tracks for the rest of my life. I walked along the platform to the exit, when a man stopped me and asked me if my name was Christy Fleming. I looked up at this tall man and realised that he was a Garda. I took off across the platform, jumping onto the tracks, running as fast as I could. But to no avail, because some of the station staff held on to me till he caught up.

I cried so much, begging them to let me go home to see Mam, but they refused. It seems that once I had been missing from the school for three days it was guessed that I might just head for Dublin, and the Gardaí were watching out for me (anyone would think that I was a serial killer). I was so angry, because my home in Townsend Street was at the back of Pearse Street Garda Station, where they were now holding me. But the Gardaí refused to travel that short distance to tell Mam that I was being held there, only yards away from my dream of freedom.

I was interrogated about our escape and whether I knew the whereabouts of Ginger and Darkie. I was hoping that they were still on the run, but there was little I could tell them because I honestly didn't know. I was hungry, cold and utterly exhausted from walking so far and from the mental strain of all the fear and worry of trying to get home to my mam. The thought of being taken back to the hellhole of Upton had my heart pounding in absolute terror. They had no sympathy, just kept shouting at me, "Why did you do it, and where are the other two? You'd better tell us if you want get a meal."

My head was splitting from all the shouting and bullying. It felt like being back in the school again. I begged and begged for them to let my mam come to see me. I cried like I never cried before, but they wouldn't listen.

I was escorted by a plain-clothes Garda on to the Cork train, and he said that he would be watching me closely all the way and that I would not be going anywhere without him. I thought to myself that no matter where I go, the bullying just continues.

The train stopped at Portlaoise Station, where the woman had fed me and collected money for my ticket: the only place that I'd felt kindness in so long. Watching through the carriage window at people coming and going, I wondered if somebody in the café had phoned the Gardaí to inform on me? This possibility left a bitter taste in my mouth.

For the rest of the journey, I leaned my head against the window, seeing again the places that I had rested during my journey to Dublin. I saw the stations where I had stayed overnight, and cried. I wished it would rain so nobody could see my tears.

As the train passed through the tunnel into Cork station, I was overwhelmed with fear at the thought of who would be there waiting to bring me back to the hateful Upton Industrial School.

six

BACK TO HELL

We pulled in to Cork station at 7pm. I was terrified getting off the train. I knew what was going to happen to me, but there was little I could do. Upton was worse than a prison. At least in prisons they have rights, they have privileges, and the staff do not beat prisoners. I was terrified of the beating I knew I would receive when they got their hands on me.

There, waiting on the platform, I saw Brother Peter, the evil man feared by all the boys in the school. He stood there with a face like thunder, full of hate. I almost wet myself. The Garda handed me over to him, said a curt goodbye, turned and walked away. I cannot put into words what my insides felt like, as I knew that I had to travel all the way back to Upton with this monster. What might he do to me?

He grabbed me by the arm, dragged me out of the station and pushed me into a white van. Not a word was spoken on the journey, and he just glared through the windscreen, completely ignoring me.

The next morning I was taken to the school office to face the music and take my punishment. I waited for Brother Peter to take out the cane or leather strap, but this didn't happen. Instead, he told me to remove my shoes and remain standing.

Suddenly he raised his leg, then without warning came down hard on my right foot. The pain shot up through my body and out the top of my head. I grabbed my foot and started hopping about, screaming in agony. He screamed even louder at me, "Shut up and put your two feet on the ground!" When I was finally able to stand, again without any warning, he repeated the same punishment on my left foot. It was the worst pain I ever experienced. I couldn't stand and collapsed to the floor.

He glared down at me and shouted, "Now, you won't be running anywhere, you little Dublin bowsie."

I couldn't stand without falling over and had to be helped to the infirmary. They told me that my big toe was broken, and two toes on my left foot were badly sprained, resulting in a week's bed rest there. I was not brought to a hospital because it would be too difficult to explain away my injuries. How have so many people stayed silent about these assaults? I will never, ever understand or forgive them.

It was a regulation that any punishment had to be entered in a punishment book. I often wondered if my beatings were entered in that book. I doubt it.

I was depressed to the point of taking my own life. At fourteen and a half years old, I was condemned to live here until I was sixteen. I wasn't sure if I would make it.

I limped around for several weeks until my toes didn't hurt any more. Even though I never had the correct treatment that I needed for a broken toe, I somehow got by. Once again, they shaved my head and put me back working in the boiler room. I was posted there up to the day of my final release.

Ginger and Darkie were on the run for almost ten days before they were captured and returned to the school. Strangely enough, they were found together because Ginger had got scared walking around on his own and went looking for me, knowing I was heading for Dublin. When he failed to find me, he made his way back to the hospital where Darkie had just had his ankle strapped up. The hospital staff had already informed the school to come and collect him. Ginger persuaded Darkie to do a runner.

They decided to head for the North of Ireland to try to find Darkie's brother. They had a hard time on the journey and were finally caught in Dundalk. Needless to say, they paid dearly for running off, and, when I had a chance to talk to them days after they returned, both of them swore never to run away again. I felt the same. The most painful of all for me was to have been within walking distance from Mam and not get to see her. This stayed with me the rest of my life.

There's one night that will stay in my memory forever. It was 8pm. I had just finished banking down the boiler and headed for the dormitory to my bed. I was totally exhausted, having worked in the boiler room since 5.30am, and my hands were sore from cutting up lorry and bus tyres all day. As I got to the dormitory there were four boys standing outside Brother Peter's bedroom, situated at the top end of the dormitory. Two of them were my age and the other two lads were about ten or eleven. Brother Peter, being the Brother who broke my toes, instructed me to stay with these boys. I pleaded that I was unable to stay awake, as I was so tired. He ran at me and punched me on the back of my head shouting at me, "Do what you're told.

Have you not learned your lesson yet?"

We were taken downstairs and out to the front of the school, where there was a parked van. We were told to get into it. As it moved off, I asked one of the older boys if he knew where they were taking us. He giggled nervously saying that I would soon find out.

We were driving for about ten minutes when the van pulled up outside a farmhouse. Brother Peter knocked on the door and then shouted at us to get out of the van and follow him inside. We were given soft drinks, cakes and biscuits, and soon after I passed out.

When I woke up I had no clothes on and I had no idea how long I had been unconscious, but I was lying on a bed. When I became fully aware of my situation, I kicked off, shouting at an old priest who was taking photos of me. I tried to jump up but one of the Brothers and a man I never seen before forced me back down on the bed. They dragged me to the floor and bent me over the back of a wooden chair with my head face down facing the seat. One of the Brothers knelt in front of me and held my arms firmly, preventing me from moving.

The farmer raped me first. I knew him, as I spent many a time working on his farm. Then Brother Peter took his turn while the old priest continued to take photos. I did everything I could to get away from them, but I was too weak and dizzy and had no strength. This was the same priest who we were forced to go to for Confession. In the Confession box, he would ask us, "Do you have bad thoughts?" He always wanted to know if we masturbated and what we were thinking about when we did.

I screamed loudly with pain and cried as I never

cried before, until they finally stopped and allowed me to get dressed.

The other boys were in a different room and I could hear a lot of crying. I believe that they had put something into our drinks and then these monsters had raped us without a shred of compassion or decency. These were supposed to be men of God. They were not even human. They were devils out of hell, dressed up as God's people.

As I am writing this, I can still smell the filthy, stinking sweat of those evil beasts, and I would rather be dead than allow myself to be caught in that situation again. I would cut my own throat without hesitation rather than allow myself to be abused like that again. I was the only one of the boys who kicked off and fought them. The other boys had been through this before.

I was in a lot of pain and there was blood leaking from my bum for days. I was terrified to go to the nurse to be checked just in case she would report back to them and I could end up getting another beating. After a couple of days, the bleeding stopped and the pain eased. I firmly believe the reason they never selected me again for their fun was because I would have made too much of a racket.

For days, I was acting like a zombie, refusing to talk to any of my friends. I was so depressed and ashamed, but I knew I had to carry on. Some days were like this, dark and never-ending, and the only way to get through them was to remember that every day ends.

Brother Peter never liked me and made no attempt to hide it. At every opportunity he would find some reason to punish me and punch me in the head. Other boys suffered the same fate. He was feared by all.

One morning, I was told that Ginger and three other boys had been called to the office for punishment. It appears that there was a fight in the play yard and, as they were being separated, Ginger took a swing at one of the Brothers. Hitting at one of the Brothers was serious stuff. When I got back to the dormitory that night I noticed that Ginger's bed had no bedclothes and there was no sign of him anywhere. I was really concerned for him. The following morning, I enquired where he was and they told me that he had been transferred to another school. When I asked another Brother about Ginger he told me that he had run away again and they were looking for him.

Each night I went to bed I kept hoping that I would see my best friend back in his bed but he never appeared. I kept asking questions and got the same answers every time. They never made any sense. Brother Peter gave me a few more hidings for what he described as disrespect towards the staff, as I never stopped asking about where he was. I knew they were being evasive.

I never did see Ginger after that, and, to this day, I always look out for him, hoping that he really did run away and that he got to the UK. I may never know what happened to my great friend.

seven
DEPRESSION

One year to go until my release and I really thought I would never make it. I was depressed and couldn't get that sexual attack by those perverts out of my head. It was bad enough to be abused by the Brothers and even that old evil priest, but I couldn't bear the thought that they brought me outside of the school to share me and the other boys with their civilian friends.

If there had been three in the room with me, how many of them were there in that house altogether on that horrific night? With so many involved, how could this be kept secret?

The beatings were something I could get over, but the idea that these animals had raped me made me feel deeply ashamed. I felt it was my own fault and that I should have done more to stop them, but in reality, what could I have done? I was only a young child dwarfed by these large strong adults who could knock me out with one blow.

There were several other Brothers who never hurt us or sexually abused us, but they must have known what was going on. Shame on them also! Their silence made them just as guilty. If only one of them had spoken out, many young boys could have been saved from such awful degradation.

Abuse by the older boys was not regarded by staff as serious and was downplayed to protect the reputation of the school. The man who sharpened the knives we used for cutting the big tyres told us this. He was a nice person, and always advised us to stay clear of the bullies who were also abused by the Brothers and who, in turn, became abusers themselves. I never told him about my abuse.

The Department of Education did not carry out its responsibilities with regard to supervising the school or protecting children. Food, clothing and accommodation were below acceptable standards. Boys were hungry, and, even when we got food, it was of inferior quality to that eaten by the Brothers and priests. I knew what they had to eat as, occasionally, I had to serve them. Most of the time, our tea wasn't hot enough. The porridge was lumpy and salty, and bread and dripping was never enough for a main meal.

Punishment and fear would have impeded learning, but in truth there was never any real effort to teach us to read or write. Like many boys, I was never allowed to attend any lessons. I was put to work, without any choice in the matter. We never had a chance to learn or study as we would have done in a normal school. Isn't it ironic that the judge sent me here because he wanted me to learn? I would have learned more at home in Dublin, even if I only went to school one day a week. What a sick joke!

The remote location of the school contributed to the emotional trauma of the boys. Not being able to interact with people outside the school prevented us from being prepared to go out into the outside world. We didn't know how to fit in with the rest of the community.

I worked very hard in that boiler room, to the extent that I lost weight and always felt unwell. The abuse kept going through my head and I didn't know how to process it. I made a decision one day to make that turmoil in my head go away for good.

There was a large barn opposite the boiler room where we stored the tyres and the strips of leather. One day, I went in there, telling the other boy I worked with, Paddywhack, that I was going to tidy it.

For days I had thought about hanging myself, and the more I thought about it the more I embraced it, knowing all that pain and torment in my head would be gone forever.

There was a ladder leading to the upper level of the barn, and when I climbed up I threw a rope around a beam and tied the other end around my neck. I sat with my legs dangling over the edge for about five minutes, preparing to drop myself. Five minutes passed, then another five, then I got so distraught that I burst out crying. My crying turned to anger because I couldn't make myself jump. I wanted to jump so badly. I needed to jump to make all the pain and shame in my head go away. But I couldn't. I remember thinking that I would not be the first boy to hang himself in this place over the past fifty years or more.

Thoughts of my mam, my friends in Dublin and my family crowded my mind, pushing me further into a deep depression. I knew that I could never share all of this with them. It was then that Paddywhack called out to me: "Christy, Christy. You OK Christy? Brother Peter is coming around."

I quickly removed the rope from around my neck and hurried back to the boiler room. I went back to work, bringing the steam pressure up for the heating and the kitchen, as the fire had died down while I had been in the barn. Brother Peter wanted to know why the steam pressure had dropped. He began shouting, "Where were you? What were you doing?" He was irate, to say the least. This time he punched Paddywhack several times, demanding that we get the steam up in double quick time or that he would be back and the next time the consequences would be severe.

Paddywhack was left semi-conscious from the beating, so it was left up to me to build up the steam again. I suppose I was lucky that I wasn't beaten. I felt sorry for Paddywhack as he was only watching out for me while I was in the barn.

Brother Peter made many visits to the boiler room, and each time he would get me out of the way by telling me go the barn to tidy it. After several of these visits, I realised what he was really up to. Once, I sneaked back from the barn and I could see he had taken Paddywhack to the rear of the huge boiler. They were having sex. Shocked, I ran quickly back to the barn without being noticed.

I tried to ask Paddywhack what was going on without telling him what I had witnessed. He had replied, "Stay out of it, Christy!" I continued to question him and eventually he told me what was going on. He explained that he had already spent eight years in the school and was looking forward to his sixteenth birthday in eight months' time. To survive here he learned that he had to put up with Brother Peter's brutality. Brother Peter made his time in the school easier than others, but it came at a very high price.

"When I finally get out of here," said Paddywhack, "I'm coming back to give that bastard a right hiding."

Brother Joe, a short lump of man in his late fifties was also one to be feared. He would patrol the play yard looking for any excuse to beat us up. He had lost the top of the thumb on his right hand, and we knew he was in a bad mood when he would close up his four fingers tightly in a fist, and twirl the half thumb around. He caught Darkie and me smoking one day. It was too late when we spotted him running at us with his face in a twisted rage. He was shouting so loud and fast that we couldn't understand what he was saying. But we knew that it was bad news for us.

First, he got Darkie by the hand that held the cigarette and crushed his fingers around it. Poor Darkie let out a scream as it burned right into his palm. Then, without warning, Brother Joe swung his fist and caught him on the side of the head. He collapsed to the ground. I could only stand there in utter disbelief and watch what was happening. He gave Darkie two kicks as he lay on the ground.

He then turned to me. I could see the hate in his eyes, and I didn't know if I was going to survive this one. He ran at me, swinging his fists, and boxed me on both sides of the head. I thought that it would fall off my shoulders. I fell onto the hard ground in a heap. He stood over us like a raging bull, snorting and panting like a man possessed. I closed my eyes, pretending to be unconscious. I could hear his heavy footsteps walking away, so I opened one eye to try and see where he was going. He quickly came back and threw a bucket of water over us shouting, "Get up, get up, or there will be more of the same!" Standing very shakily on our feet, he then ordered us to go to the nurse to be checked for black eyes and sore heads. How thoughtful of him.

So many boys were sexually abused and then threatened with violence if they resisted. We were vulnerable in this hellhole with no one we could talk to and nowhere to run. We couldn't write to our families to tell them about the abuse, because all letters were monitored, in and out.

I often thought about my attempt to hang myself and felt glad that I never made that jump, thanks to Paddywhack alerting me to Brother Peter. I made up my mind that I would stick it out and even fight, if necessary, to get to my sixteenth birthday.

During my last few months, I spoke to several boys about what was going on. One, named Danny, told me that I was lucky to have been taken to the farmhouse only once. He was taken several times to what he called The Outhouse of Hell. I met up with Danny in London in 1999. Sadly, he died in 2002. R.I.P.

One day in December 1959, I was told to get to the showers and then report to the Brother's office. When I got there the Brother handed me some clothes and told me to change into them. With a smirk on his face he said, "Cheer up, Fleming. You're going home."

I couldn't believe it. I got very emotional and struggled to hold back the tears. I found out later that Mam had been fighting for a year for my early release, so they had decided to let me go three months before my 16th birthday. During my worst days, the thought of my mam's love kept me sane and I knew that she would always be fighting for me. She knew very well what these institutions were like. She had spent many years of her childhood in one that was managed by nuns.

Brother Peter accompanied me to Cork city. During the journey he never stopped advising me to forget the schools and move on with my life as an adult. This wasn't the first time that I had heard these words. He had started telling me the same thing over the past three or four months. He had almost been nice. And I mean almost! But he couldn't keep his true self hidden. I now realise that he knew Mam had been fighting for me to get home to her, and he was just trying to soften me up so that I wouldn't talk about all that had happened.

He got very annoyed when I asked him what happened to Ginger and made no attempt to answer. That only increased my worries about what had really happened.

He took me to the train station and remained on the platform while I boarded the train, continually stressing that I should put the last years behind me and get on with my life. As the train was moving off, he waved to me and I completely lost it and shouted out to him, "Fuck off, you dirty bastard!"

I only said that when the train was moving because I knew he wouldn't be able do anything about it. It was the best feeling I had had in years. I wished I could have kicked his arse. He called out furiously, "You will end up in prison, Fleming!" I thought to myself, "You first, I hope!"

I was seated opposite a middle-aged couple, and the woman told me off for using bad language to a man of the cloth. I couldn't help myself and started to tell her and her husband what that so-called man of the cloth did to me. I shouldn't have bothered because the next thing she did was slap me across the face, saying, "How dare you talk like that about a priest!"

I told her he wasn't a priest but a Rosminian Brother. It was then that I made my mind up not to tell anyone about the school. How could anyone believe me?

As for telling my mam, that was definitely out of the question. She was true to her faith and I had no desire to take that from her. It was 1959, and I was convinced that in this Catholic country if I tried to tell anyone about what happened to me, they would accuse me of lying or being insane and would commit me to a mental home or worse.

When I look back at that time, nobody would believe what was going on in those schools. When these people of the cloth, priests and Brothers, were occasionally forced to admit to abusing children under their care and guidance, the Church simply sent them to other locations. The cycle of their sexual abuse of children simply continued at different locations.

The issue of clerical sexual abuse has emerged through many investigations and reports, including the One in Four investigation, which included results of a search through the archives in Rome. It dealt with seven sexual abusers who worked in Upton.

Even though it was great to be home with my family, I had brought an awful lot of emotional baggage with me and little else. I could barely read or write, I had a mouth full of rotten teeth due to neglect and I had certainly lost my faith in the Church.

I was met by my aunt Maggie at Kingsbridge Station

as Mam was working. We got a bus to my home where my two brothers and my twin sister Margaret were waiting to greet me. The whole day was full of questions, and I was both excited and emotional. Now I was home in Dublin and couldn't be happier. I thought a lot about my experience in those industrials schools, but decided to try to take note of what Brother Peter had said, "Move on and leave the past behind."

I struggled to do that but still suffered greatly from the terrible memories, and was subject to terrifying nightmares. Mam became very upset because I refused to attend Mass or go to Confession. It was really difficult to make her understand my reasons without telling her all about the sexual abuse, rape and physical punishment I had endured. I could never disclose those details to her.

At first, I used to pretend to her that I was going to Mass, when in fact I would go for a walk around the city for an hour. After my experience in the schools with those men who were supposed to be men of God, I couldn't follow the Catholic religion. If I needed to believe in a God, I would search to find a kind, caring one and I would talk directly to him – no middle man.

eight

ARMY DAYS

I decided I would join the army on my sixteenth birthday, even though I knew that I would have to pretend I was seventeen. I didn't have many options for work. My background in the industrial schools was against me. Most employers regarded boys from these schools as untrustworthy and risky to take on. I was told by a regular soldier who lived near me that the army was looking for recruits. Despite that, I was worried that even the army wouldn't accept me.

I was so excited about joining up. It was on my mind for weeks before my birthday. It was March 1960 when I made my way to Collins Barracks in Dublin, near the Phoenix Park, to ask if I could enlist. They gave me a thorough medical check, but I failed the eyesight test and was turned away.

I was devastated, and at the same time angry with myself for not realising that my eyesight was so bad. I knew that I had to come up with a plan and try again. For the next week, I walked all over Dublin checking out the eye test charts at every optician I could find, taking note of the sequence of letters. I was surprised to see that pattern was the same on all of them, so I learned them off by heart over a couple of days. This time I stayed clear of Collins Barracks and made my way to Cathal Brugha Barracks in Rathmines.

As expected, I was given a medical and an eye test and this time passed with flying colours: time well-spent visiting the opticians! I was shown into the recruiting sergeant's office. It was a place that reeked of authority, and memories of terrible experiences with controlling people haunted me as I waited. But here, at least I could to sit down while I was waiting. My brain began to work overtime with negative fears and worries. Finally, a big, strong soldier came in and sat down across from me, and started to read some papers on the desk. I was sitting there staring at him when he looked up and stared right back at me saying, "I'm sorry son, we have a bit of a problem here." My heart started to pound inside my chest. I thought that he had caught me out lying about my age.

I could see his face soften a little. He must have seen the fear on my face. "It's okay, son," he said, "but you are half an inch too short for the army."

He said that I was only five foot three-and-a-half and I needed to be five foot four to join. My eyes began to fill and I had to struggle to stop myself from crying. He saw how upset I was and told me not to worry. He agreed to let me go through, but told me that if it had been the next day, I would never have made it. It seems that he was not the recruitment sergeant but was standing in for him while he was attending a funeral. I was very lucky to have met a kind person that day. The army took me on, despite knowing that I came out of an industrial school. I was posted to the Number 2 Platoon, 2nd Battalion to begin my recruit training.

I found the army training and discipline easy

compared to my time in the industrial schools. At least here we had fun when we were off duty, without the fear of someone coming in to shut us up, or hand out some form of punishment. The food was good and there was always enough of it. I began to feel like a human being again and loved it.

The training was hard, but beneficial, and having great friends in my platoon became a blessing in my new life. The marching, obstacle courses, physical training, shooting and night exercises were all a part of us bonding into a tight unit. We built up a strong rapport and could depend on each other's support. Now, for the first time in my life, I knew what the word comrade really meant. Sure, there were some really tough times in my training, but I was never so happy. I couldn't wait for my passing-out parade and moving on to the challenges of my army career.

On the weekends that I wasn't on guard duty, I managed to find the time to visit my mam. She was very proud of me, but she was adamant that I wasn't to volunteer to go to the Congo. She was very aware of the Irish lads who had recently been killed in an ambush there. She would say, "You are far too young to be sent to the Congo."

However, I was delighted to find that I had been selected for a special training course to prepare us for the Congo with the 1st Infantry Group. This consisted of two companies: 'A' Company from the Eastern Command and 'B' Company from the Southern Command. We were told that not all of us on the course would be guaranteed selection. I made my mind up to complete every task to the very best of my ability, and obey any order given. I was determined to be selected.

The training was hard, and a large part of it took place in the Dublin mountains. Most of it was fun, especially the part where we would crawl up the hills and charge and stab sandbags with fixed bayonets. I enjoyed it all, and this type of training was new to me. It felt like we were training to go into battle, with sergeants and corporals telling us how important it was to be prepared for a war situation. We also had lectures explaining the difficulties and the political situation in the Congo. I kept this very quiet from my mam because I knew she was quite capable of getting in touch with the barracks to block my chances of going.

At the end of the intense training, I was one of twelve who was turned down. At first, I was devastated, but I was now a stronger person and I did not let it upset me. I was advised to volunteer for the 36th Battalion, which I did.

Three days before the 1st infantry group left for the Congo, my sergeant walked into the billet and told me to pack. I would be going to the Congo in three days' time. It appears one of the lads cried off sick and I was selected to replace him.

Even though she wasn't happy about it, Mam agreed to sign the form allowing the army to post me overseas. She knew I was happy as a soldier, and I think she always felt guilty about my detention in the industrial schools. She had no need to feel guilty, as I never blamed her. I blamed the day school at Westland Row Christian Brothers for starting that chain of events by bringing me to court all those years ago.

I never felt so proud as I did that day when my

mam signed the form. I made a point of meeting up afterwards with my friends in the flats to tell them that I was going. Some of the lads were concerned because of the nine Irish soldiers who had been killed in that famous Niemba ambush. We went to the cinema that same evening and from there we made our way to the Lido café in Pearse Street to play music and hang out. I left my friends around 11pm and made my way back to Cathal Brugha Barracks.

The following morning, I was sent to the dentist to have my teeth checked and, against my wishes, he insisted on removing two of them. He gave me no choice, and I can only describe him as a seventy-year-old butcher who should have been long put out to pasture.

I went from the butcher-dentist to the army doctor. He started with my left arm and, without warning or fuss, just stuck a needle in it as hard as he could. I jumped back a little and one of the medics caught me and told me to stand still. The doctor then turned me around and he did the same to my right arm. I went to walk away thinking that I was finished, but he then spoke the only words that I had heard coming out of his mouth since I came into the room, "You're not finished yet."

I looked around and he had a small object with little sharp metal teeth that he used to scrape my upper arm twice, putting some liquid on the scratches. I found out later that it was for smallpox as there was an epidemic in the area we were being deployed to. I then had several other injections against various tropical diseases.

Most of the lads had their injections weeks before

and didn't have a problem on the day we left for the Congo. But the pain in my arms from the injections and the soreness in my gums from the teeth extractions made mine a very uncomfortable journey to Africa.

Anyway, I survived, and the painkillers got me through the next twenty-four hours.

I was a little concerned when I had to sign a form, which apparently was a will: I was only seventeen! This spooked me for a while as I remembered seeing the reports of the large funerals for the soldiers killed in Niemba. For a minute my mind was full of fear, and I wondered if maybe I wouldn't be coming back.

My arms were still very sore that day we left for the Congo. But, with so much excitement building up within me, I didn't worry too much about it. I was ready for whatever I had to face, good or bad.

According to rumour, our first location would be Jadotville, but shortly before we left it was announced that we were being sent to the province of South Kasai.

On the day of our departure we were driven in army trucks to Baldonnell Aerodrome where we had a meal. We were then lined up, handed a little bag of rations and marched out onto the runway.

We all gasped when we saw the size of the big four-propeller plane in front of us, with two large ramps going right up into what looked like a gaping mouth. This was an American Globemaster and I couldn't believe that this huge plane could get off the ground.

To be honest, I was more scared of flying than I was about going the Congo. We stopped off at Tripoli American airbase for twenty-four hours, where, for the first time, I started to feel the heat, which wasn't helping me to cope with the reaction to the injections. I kept quiet about feeling sick in case they would send me back.

The next day we landed in Kamina airbase in Katanga. There was another civil airport in Kamina, but this one was purely military. Kamina is the capital city of the province of Haut-Lomani in the Democratic Republic of Congo.

My sergeant noticed that I was unwell, so he instructed me to report sick, which I did. The army doctor could not understand why I didn't report my illness sooner, so I told him that I was afraid they would send me back home. My old insecurities still haunted me.

He joked, "So you thought the army was going to arrange a plane especially to bring you back home?" We laughed and he gave me anti-nausea pills. He said that the reaction from the injections would wear off in a few days.

We were based in Kamina and stayed there for a little over two weeks due to a number of other soldiers also taking ill after the smallpox vaccination.

The 1st Infantry group was the first Irish formation to be armed entirely with the new F.N. fully automatic rifle and the Swedish 84mm recoilless rifle, which were unlike the .303 Lee Enfield rifle that had to be cocked each time to fire single rounds. We were trained to be a hard-hitting, highly powered, independent, self-contained unit.

*'Passing Out' at Cathal Brugha barracks, 1960
(Christy, back row, fourth from right)*

nine

SOUTH KASAI

It took three long days by train to reach South Kasai. When we arrived at the station in Luputa, we were met with suspicion by the Kanioka tribe. They differed from the Baluba tribe, which we came across in Kamina, in that they were very tall and thin. One of them approached me and began to feel my hair, which I thought strange, until I learned later that we were the first group of white soldiers they had ever seen. They stood staring at us. It felt very strange and a little unnerving.

A battalion of Ghanaian troops, with 'A' Squadron in support, had previously occupied the eastern sector. Their patrol area ran from the Lubilash river on the borders of Katanga to Tabacongo in Lulua territory. The Company headquarters was in Luputa. The unit had reformed on June 17, and had taken over the entire South Kasai sector, which consisted of an area of 6,000 square miles.

Within this area we would be responsible for guarding a stretch of over 60 miles of railway line. The railway was the main supply artery from Elisabethville to Port Franqui, and to the sea at Matadi. Along this line was transported a large proportion of the supplies for Katanga to the east and for South Kasai itself. This required security patrols on both the railway and the roads.

We had to provide security at least once a week for hundreds of refugees travelling along that line to and from tribal areas. It ran along the borders of Baluba and Kanioka territories and also between the Lulua and Baluba tribes. These tribes were traditional enemies, and any relaxation of vigilance on our part could mean a flare-up of tribal wars.

It was hard work driving down the red dust paths they called roads, and sometimes we had to spend the night in the bush without tents or any form of comfort.

We had many requests from local government officials to deploy to a battle zone between tribes to stop fighting. We witnessed villages being burnt down, and saw the awful injuries and killings and the utter fear and despair amongst the women and children.

All the wonderful training that we had completed back home could never, ever have prepared us for this type of carnage. It was a recent attack by one of these tribes that tragically caused so many Irish UN casualties.

Railway duties required that a full section of ten troops had to be provided for each train journey, and there were a minimum of three of these per week. Most of our sorties lasted forty-eight hours, but could also last up to four days. Quite often a train guard came home at 6am and had to stand guard around the camp again that night from 6pm until 6 the following morning.

Private Gallagher and I would be posted on the front of the locomotive, one on each side. The reason we were positioned there was to enable us to view a

Kanioka tribe from South Kasai

President of the secessionist state of Katanga (1960-1963), Prime Minister of the Democratic Republic of The Congo (1964-1965), Moïse Tshome, with tribesmen

long stretch of the rail line ahead. It travelled between ten and fifteen miles per hour.

On one occasion, we spotted someone on the track about three hundred yards ahead, so we ordered the driver to stop while we went to investigate. We approached the interloper with caution as we were not sure if he was armed, had explosives, or if there were more people hidden in the bush, waiting to ambush.

He was very intent on what he was doing, and we were almost upon him before he looked up. He bolted off into the bush. We gave chase and Gallagher found a burst of speed from somewhere, got close enough to grab him by the arm and wrestled him to the ground. Despite being held by both of us he continued to fight, kicking and trying to bite us. I was surprised that he resisted so persistently. He only gave up when we eventually pointed our rifles at him, and raised his arms above his head. We dragged him up off the ground and started to walk him back to the train, when the corporal and two more of the detail came running towards us. The corporal began to question him and, as he could speak English, we got a lot of information.

He wasn't one of the local tribesmen, but was an officer in the government army, and, when searched, we found a small amount of explosives on him. We were lucky to have seen him, as he was about to blow the rail tracks to prevent tribesmen from travelling into his area. We took him prisoner and he remained under guard until we handed him over to the authorities in Luputa. That was the last we saw of him.

We camped out on the tracks that night as the line had to be fully checked in case more explosives had been planted. A normal journey was slow and painful before this happened, but the next morning we had to travel at half that speed. That is how I got to spend four days on a rail track in Africa.

It brought back memories of my four days walking along the tracks of the Cork to Dublin line. Could I ever have dreamed of such a coincidence?

Trench at Katala Barrier, September, 1961, Kamina. It was usually so dark at night that we prayed for sheet lightening to light up the jungle so we could see the enemy

ten

DIGGING IN

We were living behind a barbed-wire enclosure in Luputa surrounded by bushland. It was about the size of a football pitch and, for our own security, we dug trenches all around the edges. Digging these trenches was very difficult as the ground was as hard as rock. The heat was suffocating and the sweat rolled off us.

We had to man these trenches and patrol the perimeter twenty-four hours a day, never leaving the enclosure except to go on patrols. The conditions were primitive. We sometimes slept in damp pigsties under leaking tents, and at other times in the trenches. Both options were miserable, especially during the tropical rains. Sometimes it would rain for a week without stopping. We often spent hours in wet clothes. Rain gear did give us some initial protection, but, such was the severity of the downpours that it was often impossible not to get drenched.

We had a problem with snakes that regularly wriggled their way into the trenches, especially at night. Big snakes were not so bad because we could spot them and deal with them, but the small ones were more dangerous because it was difficult to detect them. Lizards were also unwelcome visitors. They were everywhere and, although the majority were

Baluba tribe from Luputa, South Kasai, July 1961

*Private Gregory Leech (right) and an unknown soldier in a trench,
Luputa, Kasai, September 1961*

harmless, some of them were poisonous and we were told to be careful of their bites. We hadn't a clue which were which. As far as we were concerned, all of them were dangerous and it was safer to kill any that we saw near us.

Private Jock McMarlow was resting on a stretcher when one of these poisonous lizards crawled underneath him. He jumped up, grabbed a shovel and managed to scoop it up with the intention of throwing it outside the tent. He got the fright of his life when the lizard ran up the handle of the shovel forcing him to drop it quickly. Hearing Jock shout, we all jumped up off our beds and instinctively grabbed our weapons. We killed it with the butt of our rifles. Poor Jock wasn't the better of it for days.

Our unit at Luputa went on many water patrols. On every one we met roadblocks by the Baluba tribes, and most of the time we managed to negotiate our way through, only to encounter the same thing on our return journey. In the beginning there would be no more than a dozen lightly-armed natives. As time went on, they increased in numbers and became better armed, so we increased our patrols also. We now went on patrols of two full sections comprising twenty soldiers each as a precaution.

There was such a shortage of water that a patrol to collect it was a necessary part of our daily routine. On one of these collection sorties, about four miles out from camp, we came across a roadblock. As usual, the Balubas had used felled trees, but this time they had built the barrier much larger than normal. When we stopped, they appeared from both sides of the road and out of the bushes. Tensions between the tribes had been building over a number of days but, unfortunately, they didn't seem to understand that we were only there to help them keep the peace between the locals and to try to save lives.

Talk about being piggy in the middle!

There must have been fifty or sixty of them carrying bows, arrows, spears, machetes and pieces of wood with nails sticking out of them. Some of them had old single-fire rifles.

Bear in mind that most of us were only seventeen or eighteen years old and had never seen a black man before we came to the Congo. Until today, we had only seen them in small groups.

As we looked down from the truck at their manic eyes, heavily painted faces, some with unbelievably badly shaped and rotten teeth, they seemed like utterly wild men. The situation got very heated and it was obvious that they had either been drinking Simba, the local brew, or were drugged up. We had to be prepared for the worst, bearing in mind that we had lost nine Irish UN soldiers as a result of a Baluba ambush some months previously. This was on all of our minds.

They started to shout and rant at us and one of them got carried away, firing an arrow that hit the truck windscreen, narrowly missing our corporal by inches. Our sergeant approached and tried to persuade them that we were friendly and meant them no harm. It appears that they believed we were taking the side of an opposing tribe. Our sergeant failed to convince them that they were wrong.

I feared that I was going to get involved in a battle with these Balubas. I was scared and shaking until I remembered that this wasn't just about me: I was part of a section and didn't have the luxury of being afraid. My fear turned to determination and I steeled myself for whatever the outcome was going to be.

The sight of these tribesmen was enough to make anyone scared. After about ten minutes listening to them ranting and waving their weapons in the air, Sergeant Mooney ordered us to stand to.

As this made no impression on their attitude, he ordered us to fire warning shots over their heads. If anything, it made them angrier and they began shouting louder at us, waving their weapons frantically. Sergeant Mooney jumped up onto the truck, pulled out an army bag and emptied the contents onto the ground. There was a Bren gun tripod along with army cutlery and three gasmasks.

He instructed three of us to wear the gasmasks and take the front line and for the rest of the section to fall in behind us. We then fixed bayonets and took up the on-guard position. He handed another solider a tin mug, army issue, and ordered him to the centre rear of the sections telling him to hit the mug hard with his bayonet on every step as we advanced forward. He said, "Lads, just remember all those hours practicing riot drills and do exactly that and we will be okay."

Checking that we were in the correct positions, he then told us to advance forward very slowly to the beat of the rear soldier. He suspected the Balubas were very superstitious and that there was a good chance they would back down. I wasn't happy wearing the gas mask or being in the front line as we approached them. I was sweating and my vision was blurred with my breath misting the mask, but I kept my finger on the trigger, with my FN rifle set at automatic. I prayed that I wouldn't have to fire.

Private Jim Kavanagh was to my left and Private Desi Jordon to my right in the front line. The three of us didn't speak. We took very deliberate steps towards the Balubas in time with the clanking cup. As we moved forward, our three hearts pounded so hard that we didn't need any drumbeat to keep us in step.

Several of the Balubas moved towards us waving their weapons and ranting. We were outnumbered, and I was convinced we were going to be attacked. They began to move towards us, but Sergeant Mooney shouted, "As you were, keep moving forward and wait for it, wait for it!"

Private Kavanagh asked, "You OK, Christy?" I swallowed and replied, "I think so."

I wasn't OK. I was shit scared and I know most of the others were too, but we were well trained and prepared to put that training into action. Thank God for riot drills.

As we got closer to the enemy, with the sweat running down my back, I thought to myself that there was no way out of this one. At that moment, Mam came into my mind and I remembered her letters telling me that if trouble started, I was to dig a hole and hide in it.

The Balubas crossed over the blocked road to our side and it was then that I prayed that if they were going to charge, I would prefer that it would be sooner rather than later. The thought of hand-to-hand fighting these guys – especially little me, only 5 foot 3 and a half inches – no, thank you. We sure as hell didn't need that.

We were about fifteen feet from them when the leader motioned to the others to lower their arms. They stopped ranting and shouting and very slowly and quietly retreated back into the bush. We couldn't believe our luck.

The sergeant ordered us to continue as we were, but by the time we reached the roadblock they had all disappeared. I have to say that this was the nearest thing to a serious incident where so many people, tribesmen and soldiers, could have died. That wouldn't have gone down too well back at the United Nations headquarters. None of the lads, including myself, were going to hold back had the tribesmen attacked us. I still have nightmares of that day.

This incident gave me a clear insight of what our nine comrades in the Niemba ambush, months earlier, must have gone through. How scared they must have been, knowing they hadn't a chance of avoiding their fate. I felt a deep sadness within myself that night thinking and praying for them.

Sergeant Mooney's professionalism and coolness in the way he instructed us to follow the riot drills saved us from getting involved in a battle. He admitted later that he was fed up with the tribes trying to prevent us getting through. This incident had been the last straw. He explained that, had we backed down then, we would never again be able to collect water from the river. We had to be prepared to go out, fight for our water and fight our way back with it.

We held the area for almost three months, eventually occupying posts at Kele in Lulua territory, Mwene-ditu in Baluba territory and Luputa and Kasha in Kanioka territory.

eleven

ACCIDENT

When the Ghanaians moved out of South Kasai, they took away their own national transport and equipment. They had complained about the poor conditions, and eventually refused to remain in the bush posts. The head of the United Nations then ordered the sending in of the Irish troops.

This left us, their replacements, without access to military transport, and we had to wait a considerable time for the arrival of replacement vehicles from the UN. In the meantime, one of our companies had two posts over seven miles apart. The transport for the two posts consisted of one jeep, two pickups and one bullet-riddled five-ton truck. The speed of this convoy was a maximum of ten miles per hour as the jeep was in such bad mechanical condition. It slowed to a halt going up every hill and eventually, beyond repair, was abandoned. Roads were hopelessly rutted tracks and, after a few miles of driving, our faces would be unrecognisable under a thick coating of black/red powdery dust, which also penetrated our clothes.

Weapons were carried at all times, even to the dining hall, wash-up area and around the camp. Fully loaded, they were never further away than an arm's length.

One of the duties in this area was the protection of the UN plane that brought in supplies. When it was scheduled to arrive, we would rush out and surround the airstrip. Before landing, the pilot would circle the area until he saw us in position.

Once, on a water patrol, I was caught up in an accident that resulted in hospital treatment for minor injuries. The Balubas had set up a roadblock on a bend. As our truck rounded the bend, our driver had to slam on the brakes to avoid a collision. We skidded across the dirt road, and, as the truck started to lurch over onto its side, everyone grabbed on to whatever they could find to keep themselves from being thrown out onto the road. A lot of strong words were shouted.

I was sitting at the rear of the truck and, jumping clear, landed hard on my left side in the bushes. The side of my forehead struck a large branch, and I rolled down an embankment, landing heavily on my left arm. I lay there, stunned and unable to focus.

I became aware of Private Desi Jordan calling my name, "Christy, are you OK? Christy, get up. Come on, get up!" Then he called the others to come and help. I opened my eyes fully and he was looking at me, very worried. He reached down, caught my arm and helped me to my feet. There was blood coming out of my left eye and I could not use my left arm, not to mention the pounding pain in my head from hitting that branch. All of the other lads were uninjured.

Back at base, after the medic checked me out, it was decided that I had to go to the hospital in Luluabourg to be checked out further. The only way to get to a hospital from Luputa was in a small, single engined plane. The nearest thing we had to a runway was a rough open area about the size of a football pitch that was surrounded by thick jungle bush. It took three days before a plane arrived, so three days of excused duties was very welcome. But, with my arm in a sling and a painful eye, I was glad when that plane finally showed up.

We were told in advance that the plane would also be carrying the chief of the Kanioka tribe. Somehow the Baluba tribe had become aware of this, and so the landing strip had to be guarded by a full platoon. The plane circled above us, but the pilot refused to land because he could see Baluba movement in the bushes. He was advised that no harm would come to him or his passengers, and finally agreed to land. He made it clear that if the tribes attempted to attack the plane he would take off and leave me behind.

While all this was going on, I was in urgent need of going to the toilet for a 'number two'. Urgent enough that I shouted to Sergeant Mooney, "I have to go, I have go, I can't hold it." He gave me the okay, telling me to be quick because the plane was not going to hang around for long.

I ran a short distance into the bush and started to do my business when suddenly I heard grunting and movement behind me. I looked to my right and realised I wasn't alone and when I turned around I could see several armed Balubas. They were pointing at my white bottom and laughing, at the same time coming towards me. The sweat broke out all over my body as I could see that they were all armed and this was the first time in weeks that I did not have my rifle by my side. I felt very vulnerable and helpless.

I knew the plane was waiting as I could hear its engines running. Sergeant Mooney shouted at me to hurry up, "This plane won't wait for you, Fleming, get your ass up here right now!" Referring to my ass was all too appropriate! I quickly pulled up my trousers and ran as fast as I could and scrambled on to the plane with two other Irish UN soldiers. One of them was very ill with food poisoning and the other had dysentery.

We took off and we settled down for the journey. When I sat down, I felt uncomfortable and quickly realised that when I had pulled up my trousers to run for the plane, I had accidently scooped up part of my load (if you pardon the expression), and it was very messy. I was sitting right behind the pilot and it was only a matter of time before he complained about the smell.

I was so embarrassed, and came up with the excuse that the guy next to me had dysentery and couldn't control his bowels. I felt bad blaming the other soldier and, every time I think back to that day, I still feel guilty. At least the other soldier was so out of it that he wasn't aware of what I had said. When we landed I still had to face the medical staff and try to explain my predicament.

Nurses from the local hospital met us when we arrived. As they brought us inside, they began to ask questions and I noticed that one of them spoke with an English accent. I asked if I could speak to her privately. She took me into a room and I explained what happened before I got on the plane. I really thought that she wouldn't believe my story. To my relief she was quite sympathetic about it, but I could see that she was struggling to hide that lovely smile on her face. She asked me to undress and took my clothes away to be washed while I showered. It was great to feel almost human again, to have the first real wash in weeks and feel the hot water on my skin.

I was treated for my injuries. The arm was just a bad sprain and they gave me painkillers for my headache and eye injury. Two days later I was back on duty in South Kasai.

This was a godforsaken place, full of filthy, rough road tracks, surrounded by jungle bush. There were no towns and we spent most of our time in the wet, fetid trenches. Four highly dangerous Black Mamba snakes were killed in the tents in one day. In time we got used to them being around, but we still had a respectful fear of them.

After a couple of months, we were informed that we would be moving to another location. Rumours were rife, with everybody hoping that finally we would be posted to a large town or city.

An advance party of Nigerian troops arrived at the camp. It looked like they would be taking over the garrison. At last things were looking up. We would soon be out of here. Orders came that we were to prepare to be withdrawn from South Kasai and move back to Kamina. Over the three months we had been there, the shooting war between the local troops and the UN had died down. Now South Kasai was considered a safe area.

The UN garrison was not replaced there as the Nigerian advance party reported back that the posts were not suitable for soldiers to live in. The conditions were not up to any kind of living standard for humans.

The 1st Infantry Group had spent months in these conditions and had 'carried out their duties to a man' as ordered. But troops from Africa found them to be uninhabitable.

Nyunzu, Congo, 1961. We would have to sit on the tent poles when helicopters arrived, if not, the tents would take off and we would be soaked from the rain.

twelve

RETURN TO KAMINA

We were all looking forward to our new posting back in Kamina airbase. This was the only place that we lived a reasonably normal lifestyle since coming to the Congo. Little did we know what lay ahead.

We took over from the remaining battalion of Nigerians and assumed responsibility for running the installations of this huge base. It covered over a hundred square miles. There was a garrison posted to Kilubi about sixty miles away to protect the hydroelectric station supplying it with electricity. Also there were roughly one hundred Swedish troops under the command of Colonel J.C. O'Donovan, who was the base commander.

With such a huge area, there was not much time for rest due to the number of different duties that we had to carry out. But, it was a vast improvement on South Kasai. Living conditions were excellent and work was much easier. We worked in the kitchen, cleaning the accommodation, escorting officers and other officials. We did some guard duties and organised sports events.

For sixteen days Kamina was like Paradise. We couldn't believe our luck after living in the bush for months in filthy conditions among the tribes. We slept in real beds and had access to a canteen. The officers' accommodation was on the outskirts of the main base. They slept in bungalows close to the farm area at the edge of the bush.

One of the young officers asked Sergeant Mooney for two soldiers to guard his bungalow while he went to a meeting in Elizabethville. Joey Whelan and I volunteered. Sergeant Mooney looked at us suspiciously, wondering what we were up to. Joe and I were great friends. He was on his second tour of the Congo and kept me informed of the duties to avoid. Sergeant Mooney was well aware of this. Spending several hours house-sitting in the officers' quarters until after midnight was one way of being excused from guard duty around the base. We stood there 'all innocent'. Eventually he said, "Okay, go on, get a jeep and get down there and don't get up to any mischief. I know the two of you, so be careful." "Yes, Sergeant," we said, and almost skipped out the door. Another piece of heaven awaited us.

When we got there, it was not as exciting as we had hoped. The house was sparsely furnished, just a couple of chairs, a table, a sofa, a bed and a fridge. For a while we talked and played cards. It only took a couple of hours before we got bored and raided the fridge. We couldn't believe our luck when we saw so much beer in it. We drank every drop and fell asleep.

The officer returned around 2.30am to find Joey and myself sprawled out on the sofa. He woke us up but remained very calm. Quietly he told us to get out to the jeep. I thought that we were in for the jump and would be brought to the guardroom to be locked up. Instead, he drove us back to our quarters and Joey had the cheek to ask him if we could be excused from early duties, to which he replied, "You wish." Looking

Irish UN troops capture and deport Belgians, September 1961

Christy in Lupata, South Kasai, 1961

back on it the following day, we were glad that he was one of the good officers, and maybe he acted as he did knowing all the hardship we had endured for months before being posted here.

On August 27, two prisoners who were Katanganese officers were brought to the base and Joey and I had to guard them. One of them was a French mercenary. The following day more mercenaries were picked up from different parts of Katanga. In a short time, we had one hundred and fifty in the base under guard.

A large number of these mercenaries had fought in every lucrative war over the past twenty years. They formed a roving army of 'Guns for Hire', tough and completely ruthless. In addition to guarding these prisoners, we also had to round up twenty-seven mercenaries in our own area, the majority from Kaminaville town, about fifty kilometres away.

As if our normal everyday duties were not already a strain on our resources, we now had extra guard duties around their compound. Added to this, from September 2 onwards, a patrol of fifty soldiers had to make a nightly run into Kaminaville town.

Our strength on the base at this time, including the Swedish company, was roughly three hundred and forty. The mercenaries were held inside a fenced compound. They slept in huts, and guarded twenty-four-hours a day.

It was my turn to do a night patrol around the detention compound. At around 1.30am, out of the corner of my eye I noticed movement. One of the mercenaries was climbing over the fence. I pointed my rifle towards him and called out, "Get back down now or I will shoot!" He laughed out loud and shouted,

"You haven't got the balls to shoot, you're only a boy." Even though I was seventeen, I knew I looked younger, and the FN rifle must have looked taller than me.

There was no way I could let him climb onto my side of the fence because I was fully aware how well trained these mercenaries were. I shouted again, "Get back down or I will fucking shoot you!" He ignored my warning and laughed as he crossed a leg onto my side of the fence. I took aim and waited for him to put both feet on the ground. I had already decided that I was not going to kill this guy. If he came at me I would shoot him in both legs. I worked out that doing that would stop him getting too close. Once more in my young life I'm here with my heart pounding so hard I thought that it could be heard back at base.

Just before he was about to jump onto the ground, there was a burst of single shots from behind me. The mercenary quickly climbed back over to his side and ran back into his hut. The shooting came from Private Winnie Kavanagh who was also patrolling the area. He thought that I was going to be attacked and fired warning shots. I'm so glad he arrived when he did. I believe I would have shot the mercenary before he got to me. There was no question of letting him get too close. I was ready to open fire.

On many occasions my sergeant approached me saying, "Fleming, how old are you really? This time, tell the truth." He said that I looked too young to be eighteen. I eventually admitted to him that I was seventeen, but he still didn't believe me. Several of the lads also thought that I was about fifteen because I looked so young and was so short. I got fed up with their remarks and the idea that they felt they had to always watch my back. I did the same training as them and that made me just as good a soldier as they were, no matter how young I looked. However, when word got around about how I handled that late-night incident, my age was no longer a talking point.

On the night of September 13, we got the word to 'stand-to'. One of our young officers approached myself and Private Desi Jordan, requesting an escort to his accommodation, four miles away. He drove us to his bungalow and instructed us to remain outside on guard. There was no cover and we felt vulnerable, sheltering behind the jeep.

He came out, carrying bags containing his private belongings. He instructed us to get on board quickly and drive back to base. Neither of us was very happy that he put all three of us in danger just to collect his belongings. We didn't stay angry for long because soon the base came under attack from Katanga government forces, including mercenaries who had wanted the United Nations out of the country. That young officer proved to us how capable he was in conducting his duties in leadership of the highest quality. We were glad that he was among us and we would have followed him into any battle. I felt proud to be a soldier.

The following morning, September 14, a dozen of us were sent to a location on the outskirts of the base. This was used as the officers' mess and was in Base Two at Lumwe. There was a lovely swimming pool there and we looked forward to diving into it.

We were there to look after our officers and keep the building clean. On arrival, we were told that six of us would start work right away and the other six early the following day. All of those on the morning shift were brought to their sleeping accommodation and told to take the day off. Myself and another soldier from 'A' Company, whose name I think was Peter, were put into a room already occupied by six soldiers from 'B' Company and given two beds in the corner. We had a few words with the three of them that were there, and they explained what the duties were like in the building. When they left, we decided to find the other four and do something for the rest of the day.

When we met up, one of the other lads had already got a crate of Simba beer, the local strong drink. It all started off with high spirits and we had a great laugh telling silly stories. To tell the truth, after a couple of bottles I thought that everything they said was funny. I wasn't used to alcohol.

I don't know how much Simba I drank, but I don't remember a lot about the rest of that day. I have a vague recollection of someone putting me to bed.

This was an important date, as it was the night that the battle of Kamina began. For years I could never recall the full story, but in 2015, while browsing the 'IRISH UN IN THE CONGO' Facebook page, I saw a photo of the EPA building. It caught my attention and I started to chat online to Muiris de Barra who had also served with the 1st Infantry Group. By 4.30am we realised that we were both involved in that fateful night. I always wanted to know the full story as it haunted me having a blank period in my life.

The following is his account:

14 September 1961, first day of the attack on Kamina airbase

On being deployed back to Kamina airbase, I was sent to the Officer's Mess in Base Two in Lumwe to work.

It had a beautiful outdoor swimming pool, so it was in great demand. We had a room which eight of us shared for our off-duty relaxation and sleeping, six of us from 'B' Company (Southern Command) and two from 'A' Company (Eastern Command). About twenty of us were working in this huge complex. I never really got to know the two lads from Dublin as we were rarely in the room at the same time due the duties we had to fulfil.

The day of September 14 proved to be a very different moment in our lives, as we had to depend on each other.

When I got back to my room after finishing work, the younger one was already in bed and the older one was just sitting on his. I turned towards him and we said hello to each other. It just struck me that I still did not know his name.

I was unlacing my boots when I heard loud roaring from the next room and I could hear that there was a lot of commotion in the other rooms also. A soldier ran in shouting, "Get dressed quickly, and get downstairs, we must get back to our companies right away. The base has come under attack. Come on, hurry, hurry."

Within minutes, everyone was dressed, had picked up their weapons, and were heading out the door. I was just about to join them when I realised that the Dublin lad was shouting and pulling his younger friend, trying to wake him up without any success.

The Corporal who was in charge of us from 'B' Company came in through the door, again he was shouting, "What are you hanging around for? Get out to the jeep now, there is only one left out there, and we won't be waiting!" I said, "Corporal, the Dublin lad is having trouble getting his friend to wake up."

Throwing a dirty look towards them he replied, "That's their problem, they shouldn't have been drinking. I'm ordering you to get out now."

"But Corporal, if two more of our lads ran up we could lift him down, we can't leave them here."

"For the last time, Gunner, I'm ordering you to get out now, because we're leaving."

I headed for the door as ordered but, looking back I could see the desperate and yet sad look on the soldier's face. I knew that I couldn't leave. The corporal ran off downstairs and I turned back to try and help them as best I could.

With fear building up in my stomach as I heard the jeep start up and drive off, I realised that the three of us were now stranded out here on our own. By this time, we could hear all the shooting and mortar explosions from the jungle behind us. I couldn't believe that he drove off without us. I couldn't help wishing that it had been my own section corporal who had been in charge of us, because he would never have driven away and abandoned us to our fate, knowing what might happen if the enemy got to us.

I ran over to the side of the bed. "What the fuck is wrong with him, why won't he wake up?" "He drank too much Simba and wasn't used to it," he said.

"He will get us all fucking killed," I replied. I felt guilty because I don't normally swear. "I'm sorry," I said, "I'm just worried and frightened."

We tried to dress him, which wasn't easy, as he was a dead weight. We really were not very gentle, but finally got there. We pulled his web on him in a sort of way and felt that at least we now might be able to stand him up and get him walking. That failed completely as he just fell back on the bed.

Deciding that was all we could do with him for now, we headed out onto the balcony where sandbags had been built up as cover. The sound of gunfire was getting closer and we looked at each other. I'm certain that there was as much fear in my eyes as I could see in his. I figured that he was at least four years older than I was, so he would take charge.

"What do we do when they get here, will we fight or will we surrender?" he said.

Again, I felt that knot in my stomach and replied, "I heard that they don't take prisoners."

"Okay, then we must fight," he said, looking straight into my eyes.

I just nodded and whispered, "Yes."

Believing that three guns firing would be a lot better defence than two, we decided to try and wake the Dubliner up once more. As far as I can remember, Peter was the name of the guy with me and he said that the one in the bed was called Christy.

Dragging him by the arms and web belt we finally got him on his feet. It was at this moment that a mortar bomb exploded within yards of the building. All three of us jumped in the air and Christy opened his eyes, totally unaware of where he was or what had happened.

As he staggered, we grabbed him and pulled him out onto the balcony and below the cover of the sandbags. Peter got Christy's FN and put it in his hands saying with a wry smile, "At least he might pull the trigger if we point it in the right direction."

We sat there, not sure what the outcome might be, so we made a pact that if only one of us got home we would look up the others' families and tell the full story about this night.

All the time, the sound of fighting was getting closer and closer. At one stage, we did think of trying to make a run for it. But in truth, we knew that was not going to happen, as our nearest Company lines were at least five miles away and with Christy as he was, it would be much more dangerous to be out in the open.

Another mortar bomb fell very close to the building. This stirred Christy up again and he became a bit more alert. Within a few minutes, we could hear the sound of a truck heading in our direction and said to one another, "This is it, good luck!" and took up shooting positions.

We were waiting to see who got out of the truck before we started firing, when we heard a loud Dublin voice shouting out the window, "Are there any UN here, any Irish soldiers still here?" Standing up, we started waving and shouting back but he couldn't hear us due the noise of the truck and gunfire.

As he started to turn the truck, I began to panic and told Peter that I would run down and try to stop him before he drove away and that he should grab Christy and drag him, if necessary, as far as he could along the hall and down the steps.

I don't think that I ever ran as fast before or even after, as I did on that night. Every nerve in my body was tingling; I felt as if I was floating. He was just about turned and heading off up the road when I started to bang the butt of my rifle against the back of the truck.

He braked so hard that I ran into the back of it and

almost knocked myself out. I got up and peered around the side of the truck and I could see him in the door mirror looking back at me with the same fear in his eyes as I had in mine many times in the past hours.

Getting out and coming towards me, he could hardly get the words out, "Jesus you frightened the shit out of me, what are you doing here?"

Quickly I told him the story. He said he would try to back the truck as far as he could towards the door. "For fuck's sake, hurry up or we will all get caught here."

I ran back to the stairwell and I could see that Peter had dragged Christy all the way down to the last flight of steps. Running up, taking two steps at the time I said, "Well done, Peter, let's get him to the truck." Once more we were not overly gentle with him, but grabbed his webbing and hauled him down the last flight of steps. The driver was outside just opening the tailboard. Without ceremony, we literally threw him into the back while he was muttering and swearing a lot.

At this stage, another mortar landed within ear splitting distance. Christy finally sat up and became aware of what was happening. The driver started the engine and drove off like a bat out of hell towards our lines in the EPA building, which was the location of 'A' Company.

On the way, the driver told us that he went to Lumwe searching for the chaplain, as he was not at the base. He decided that he would give a last scout around for stragglers. Thank God for that.

I want to thank Gunner Muiris de Barra for allowing me to share this account of these events, and for being there to help me get out of a dangerous situation.

By the time we got to our Company lines, I was a

little bit more alert and, with a little help from Peter and Muiris, I was able to stand up, if none too steadily. I was just about to ask Peter what had happened when I saw the young officer from the previous night walking towards us.

I straightened up as best I could with Peter and Muiris on either side of me. "It's you again, Fleming. The two of you report to your section corporals!" As I walked away, with Peter watching me closely, I could hear the officer talking to Muiris. That was the last I saw or had any contact with him for fifty-five years. I wonder if I would be here today if he had not disobeyed his corporal and stayed to help Peter and me.

We found our Section just about to load into a truck. The corporal saw us coming his way and shouted, "Come on you two, hurry up, we must get out to help the Swedish Company to defend the base." I did my best to run, but it wasn't happening. Once more Peter came to my aid and said, "Pretend that you twisted your ankle, I'll back you up."

Luckily for us, the fighting at the barrier had died down and we were ordered to take up a position a bit further back as a second line of defence.

This night proved to me that I had made the right decision in joining the army. Peter showed me that having a good comrade by your side is worth more than anything. He stayed close by my side all that night and the following morning, and never complained.

thirteen

KAMINAVILLE

With so few troops available to the base commander, he had decided that Kamina could only be held by placing strong points at key places and keeping a mobile reserve at Headquarters, which would be available to help out if assistance was needed.

One of our key 'strong' points was manned by only ten men. But ten brave and willing men are a lot better to have on your side than a hundred useless ones.

There were fourteen roads and a railway line leading into the base. It had been freely acknowledged that it would require an entire brigade to successfully defend Kamina from the Congolese, who were supported by mercenaries. It was also acknowledged that, "Who holds Kamina holds Katanga".

The enemy strength in the vicinity was 1,400 troops with eight Saracen armoured vehicles. These Saracens mounted a 57mm cannon, twin machine guns and a 5-inch machine gun each, and also had long-range mortars. They completely outgunned us.

The enemy had a reserve of 2,500 men in the Kaminaville sector. On the afternoon of September 14, the Katangan troops led by mercenaries attacked, using mortars and Saracens. The first wave of the attack came up against one of our strong points at the

Kaminaville barrier. This was manned by twenty-nine Swedes with an Irish mortar section in support. The first attack was broken up, with our 84mm recoilless anti-tank gun knocking out two of their Saracens. Our mortars blew up an enemy ammunition truck containing five tons of 81mm mortar and small arms ammunition. The commander called up his mobile reserve and further attacks were also broken up.

Probing tactics, sniping and mortar fire were tried by a resolute enemy from the edge of the jungle, and the group commander moved our section and weapons to meet these. In all cases the enemy was beaten off.

Late on the evening of the 15th, between forty and fifty of the enemy infiltrated the edge of the base and occupied some houses. This was in the vicinity of the farm area where the jungle butted right up to the houses. At first light on the following morning, our platoons counter-attacked, and routed the attackers.

After a fight lasting about three hours, the enemy left three dead in the base and five rifles were captured. We came under long-range mortar fire, but our mortar crews inched forward, getting cover from our section. We kept changing our positions replying to their attacks with deadly accurate fire. Accuracy and movement were the key to our success. The enemy couldn't locate our constantly changing positions and so their fire was ineffective. I remember thinking of the very first time I discharged my weapon during the second attack on the base. I thought to myself, "Jesus, I'm no longer a combat virgin." That was one hell of a feeling, and I was very proud. It goes to show that when you're forced into a dangerous situation you are left with only one choice, that is to use the skills that you have acquired in your training.

By 8.30am, half of our platoon under Lt. McMahon were stood down and headed back to the EPA building for some food and rest. Sergeant Mooney, Corporals Roche and Pierce, with nine of us privates, were to stay at the Kaminaville barrier to give long-range gun support to the Swedish troops. We were armed with only short-range Gustaf SMGs. If we came under attack from a distance, we wouldn't be able to return fire.

Sergeant Mooney told us to get ourselves sorted and into the trenches. "Keep a good eye out for snipers and don't make any stupid mistakes," he shouted as we hurried to our posts. We prepared our weapons and ammunition and waited, with no idea what was going to happen next.

Hardly ten minutes had passed when they began to attack again. We could see them rushing out of the jungle and the road. Once more, Sergeant Mooney's voice could be heard loud and clear, "Fire at will lads, but don't waste ammo. Pick your targets."

As if there was only one hand on all the triggers, we opened fire in unison. This time I hadn't time to think about being frightened, and just got on with defending myself and my comrades. By now I was getting used to us being on 'stand to' and taking every precaution to stay alive.

As a number of the enemy had fallen to the ground, wounded or otherwise, the remainder turned and headed back to cover. In their rush to fall back, they abandoned one of their trucks in no-man's land about five hundred yards away. The shout went up, "Cease fire, save your ammo. Well done!" A couple of the Swedish troops in the trench close to ours called out,

This Swedish helicopter was very involved with us, running sorties to Kilubi dam through fierce gunfire to bring the platoon stationed there back to Kamina air base, September 1961

Building a defensive trench

"Great shooting, Irish. Thank you!"

It wasn't long before yet another attacking wave started to come at us, and the shooting started all over again. Lieutenant Minihan and his brilliant mortar section came into their own here, and laid down a blanket of accurate mortar fire. Once again, this attack was beaten off without any losses on our side, while a number of the enemy lay on the ground.

This went on for about an hour, with waves of attacks on us that we were able to hold back. Even though our FN rifles were fully automatic, we saved ammunition by firing single shots.

At last the fighting stopped, and we were told that one of us in each trench should try to rest while the other kept watch. We were very tired as we had been up all night. Desi looked really worn out, so I said that I would take the first watch. Within minutes, he was asleep and in a few more he was snoring loudly. At least with that noise I had no problem in staying awake!

I was glad when it was my turn, and I was asleep in seconds. Something began to annoy me, something constantly touching my leg. I didn't react to it, but suddenly, a snake came into my mind as part of a dream and I jumped up. "Get down, you fool, they are getting ready again!" I heard a voice yell at me. I woke to see Desi pointing out to one of their trucks in no-man's land. Knowing that it would be dark very soon, we thought that they might be building up for a big attack once night fell.

They were heading towards the truck and it looked as if they were trying to retrieve it rather than attack us. Lieutenant Minihan and his mortar crew got back into action, as they didn't want them to get their truck back. They set up the mortars to fire on it at about five hundred yards range, scoring a direct hit with the third round. The truck, with all its ammunition, exploded. I was sure that they could hear the cheers back in Dublin. What great mortar men we had!

We were really glad to have a break because it had been a hectic twenty-four hours. We had fought off five separate attacks and everyone was tired and hungry. But everyone was safe.

Word came down the line that there had been an attack on the EPA building by a jet fighter. Bombs had been dropped, and targets strafed around the building. The officers mess in Lumwe, where I had been just over a day ago, had also been targeted. A lot of different battles raged all over the base during that day, but there were no reports of fatalities on our side. As night closed in, we settled down, taking turns at sleeping and being on guard.

I woke up the following morning to the sound of gunfire and mortars exploding in the distance. "Any idea where it's coming from?" I asked Desi. "Not a clue Christy," he replied. "Sounds like it's coming from our company headquarters, but I'm not sure." I got up quickly to try and see if there was smoke rising from where the action was taking place. As I turned my head, I could see the sand in front of me popping into the air and hear the sound of a machine gun firing. I don't know how long it took me to realise that the bullets from that machine gun were striking the ground right in front of us. Looking at each other, we knew that this wasn't the time for heroics and we quickly got back down into the trench.

Once more that calming voice of Sergeant Mooney rang out shouting, "There's a machine gun just beyond the edge of the bush. Everyone keep down, the mortars will take care of them."

Corporal McCabe's mortar section engaged them, and the fifth round landed directly on the gun, killing all the crew. There were no more full-on attacks for the rest of the day. Every now and then there would be some rifle and mortar fire, but, because they stayed hidden in the bush, they were firing blind, and it was inaccurate. At around 19.00 we were relieved and brought back to company headquarters for a well-deserved meal and, finally, some real shuteye. What a seventy-two hours we had just been through!

Desi Jordan in Nyunzu, July 1961

fourteen

ATTACK

Early one particular morning, the other platoon, under the command of Lieutenant McGrath, set off for the barrier to support the Swedes once more. When they got back that night, they told us that there hadn't been any direct attacks but long range intermittent shooting. The machine gun section always replied by sweeping the area with indirect fire, while the mortar section only fired if it looked like the enemy was trying to build up an attacking force. The enemy had found out to their cost that the Irish were well trained and could shoot accurately.

A Fouga jet attacked us daily and it was difficult to defend ourselves, as we did not have the correct weapons or any jets of our own to fight it. It was a French-made aircraft, fitted with guns and capable of dropping light bombs. We fired at it with the FNs and Bren guns, but would need a lot of luck to do any damage. Our Vickers machine guns had been set up on the balcony of the EPA building to try and get a shot at it, but it always came in too low, and so it would have been dangerous to fire, as the bullets might hit our own troops in the forward positions.

We had quite an easy day, except for that bloody jet. We cleaned our rifles and other weapons after the shooting and got rid of the dry red dust that clogged them.

The Fouga was also attacking 'B' Company up around the airport building.

Gunner Muiris de Barra of 'B' Company:

It was the fourth day into the fighting when we got a break from the trenches. We were located near the corner of the control tower in a built-up sandbag post. That day we were allowed to enter the building, one at a time, to get some food. I was just about halfway to the building when I heard the roar of the Fouga jet and could see the ground being torn up. My helmet fell off and I foolishly ran back for it. I say 'foolishly' because it was only made of cardboard and painted blue, only the lining of a steel helmet, which is what we should have had for true protection. I quickly picked it up and I could see the ground where I was running to being hit by the bullets from the jet. I suppose my 'useless helmet' saved my life.

Gunner Gearoid Bucke, 'B' Company, :

We were dug into the trenches around the perimeter of the airport building and control tower. The Fouga jet was off target when he bombed and opened fire on us. We all returned fire with our Bren guns and FN rifles. He returned several days, dropping bombs while also strafing us with machine gun fire. He blew up one of our planes and killed several civilians.

The bombs dropped about fifty yards from our trenches, and we were so lucky we were not killed. It must have been all the prayers people were saying for us at home.

Irish soldiers were also fighting in Elizabethville and Jadotville, and from reports, they were also under

The railway line between Albertville and Mwene Ditu, South Kasai, 1961

attack from the Fouga jets. Where was the UN Air cover?

At the main building of the base, I was part of a section on 'stand to' behind a three-foot wall. There were holes large enough to put rifles through along the top of the wall. When we heard mortar fire very close to the building, we were at the ready.

As the gunfire got closer, I wasn't very happy, picturing a bullet coming through this hole and hitting me in the eye. I think I would have preferred a body shot any day, so I moved to the pillar at the entrance. My officer was behind the other pillar and shouted at me to get back to my post. I replied, "Sir, I'm left-handed and need to be here." I have no idea why I said that, because it didn't make much sense. The officer just nodded his head and let me stay where I was. A unit from 'B' Company flushed out the enemy, holding off the attack and forced them to withdraw from our side of the base. 'B' Company was dug in on the edge of the base and took the full force of incoming fire.

Reports had just come through that evening that the company in Jadotville had to surrender.

'A' Company, 35th Battalion were under siege inside a compound in Jadotville, surrounded by over three thousand Congolese led by mercenaries from Belgium, France, South Africa and elsewhere. Many of these Belgians had come back to the Congo after we had deported them weeks earlier.

Reinforcements of Irish, Swedish and other nations failed to get through, after our troops came under heavy ground and air fire. So much for the UN support who decided to only send ground troops, but no air cover! The UN had access to Swedish fighter jets, but in their wisdom refused to send them to defend Jadotville.

It was felt that the UN and the Irish government were prepared to allow 'A' Company to perish, by leaving one hundred and fifty-five men to their fate against over three thousand well-equipped Congolese and mercenaries. That was the feeling among many of our lads in the 1st Infantry Group. There was no possible way our reinforcements could get through without air cover. They would have had to try to cross the river at Lufira Bridge, and that was strongly defended.

'A' Company fought for their lives for five days, until they ran out of ammunition, food and water and were forced to choose between surrender or death. They were taken as prisoners on September 17, and held for six weeks, receiving rough treatment from their captors. They had fought a brave fight and showed no weakness, despite it being their first time to see action.

During this time, we continued to come under attack by the Fouga. Its primary target was the control tower at the airport. Despite the fact that initially the enemy's ordnance out-ranged us (until we captured some of their long range 81mm mortars and fired on them with their own weapons), the only casualties incurred on the base were three Congolese civilian refugees, who were killed, and an Italian air-force pilot who was wounded in the first sneak attack. Two civilian pilots were wounded in one of the later attacks when their plane was bombed whilst on the ground.

The Fouga jet that made our lives a misery, September 1961

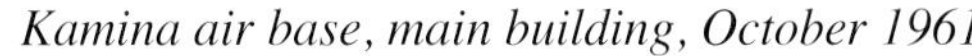

Kamina air base, main building, October 1961

fifteen

DODGING BULLETS

On the morning of September 18, our platoon was ready for a big day's work. The platoon commander Lieutenant McMahon said that we were going back to Base Two to bring all the important stores back behind our new lines. We needed to consolidate our positions, as we had been spread out over too large an area for the past few days.

Our truck pulled up at the officers' mess and we stood awaiting our orders. Sergeant Mooney looked in my direction. I tried not to look back at him as I might get a duty I wouldn't like. Then I heard his voice, "Fleming, you and your two buddies," pointing at Joey Whelan and Jock McMarlow, "Get over to the edge of the runway and stand guard. Be fully alert! The enemy is all around us here."

Joey whispered, smiling, "Christy, I must stay away from you. We are always put into the hot spots!" We walked to the runway, about three hundred yards away, keeping a wary eye on the control tower and airport buildings in the distance as we knew that they were a prime target for the Fouga jet. We patrolled up and down the side of the runway and kept a good eye on the adjacent bush for any movement, and to prevent a surprise attack on our platoon working behind us.

Out of nowhere, Jock nearly gave us a heart attack when he roared, "That fucker is coming again. Take cover!" Joey and I looked up. "Go away, you dope! That's too big," said Joey. "It must be troops coming in." Jock went quiet for a while, "But it could have been!" Joey and I laughed and carried on patrolling.

But then, when we saw a Fouga coming in over the jungle, heading for the control tower, there was no laughing. We were about fifty yards apart from each other, caught by surprise and very vulnerable in the open space. We hurridly got together and discussed what we should do if he made another pass.

As we watched, we could see that he was shooting at the control tower and 'B' Company lines. We heard two explosions and knew that he was bombing them.

He began to change direction and we headed for the cover of the bush. Joey looked over his shoulder, "Come on lads!" he shouted. "He's coming this way!" We ran towards the nearest solid building, which was the officers' Mess. It was only about three hundred yards away, but to me it looked more like a mile. The pilot flew in very low from behind us and opened fire.

I found it hard to keep up with the others because my body was shaking. I could see dust rising up about three feet to my right where the bullets ripped up the ground. I tried to run faster to keep up, when suddenly I tripped and fell flat on my face. My FN rifle went flying yards in front of me. I hit my face on the rough, sandy ground and I could feel the pain of the skin being torn off my face.

After this first pass, the jet had to swing around before he could make another circuit over us. Joey and Jock stopped running when they saw blood running down my face, and thought that I had taken a bullet.

"You OK, Christy? Are you wounded?" They ran back and helped me to my feet, and the three of us ran as fast as we could towards the building. The jet screamed towards us again, flying very low and firing continuously.

Private John Kavanagh was positioned on the balcony of the building with a Bren gun. He opened fire, giving us some cover until we reached the building safely. I threw myself behind a concrete pillar and slid down onto my rear. Joey positioned himself behind the second pillar and I can't remember where Jock was hiding, but I knew he was safe because I could hear him ranting about the jet.

On his next pass, the pilot was on target, hitting the building. The windows were blown in and debris flew all over the place. The Bren gunners on the balcony shouted at Private Gregory Leech, the jeep driver, to bring up another box of ammunition. He carried two boxes up to them. "These should do ye lads. Knock him out of the sky!" He rushed down to drive the jeep into safer cover before the Fouga made another pass. This time the fire was further away from the building. I could feel the vibration on my back from the bullets hitting the pillar. As he got closer, it looked like he was trying to take out Private Kavanagh on the balcony. The jet was so low you felt you could touch it. The three of us stood in front of the building, and, as he flew over our heads, we pointed our FN rifles, put them on fully automatic and emptied our magazines at him.

By this time there was a lot of gunfire in his direction, but we all had enough of his arrogance, thinking that he could attack us whenever he liked without reply.

We waited for another pass, hoping we could do the same again when suddenly we heard an explosion. Had he crashed into the bush? We felt like cheering. Jock said, "It's not him. There he is, heading towards Kaminaville, with smoke coming from his engine." He was definitely hit, but we were never sure if we were the ones who actually got him.

Later that day Moïse Tshombe, the President of Katanga, who had the President of the Republic removed by force, resulting in his unlawful death, announced that he had grounded the jet in order not to prejudice his talks with UN officials. Maybe his pilot had had enough.

The following day, our platoon had to go back to Base Two to finish the work from the previous day that had been rudely interrupted by the Fouga. We had a mortar section with us and we were very happy to have them.

We also had to provide protection for an Irish commandant and a major from the Swedish battalion. Theirs were the troops that we had seen arriving the previous day. They would be a huge help in protecting the base and would share our daily duties.

We could hear some shooting from time to time on the far side of the base, but nothing came our way. Later, back in the EPA building, some soldiers who had been out there informed us that Jat (Indian) troops had kept up harassing fire using their heavy armaments on likely enemy areas, so perhaps this kept the enemy at bay for that day.

If we thought that we could now just laze around and relax for the rest of that night, we were mistaken. An NCO came in and told us to get our gear and

Katanganese soldiers

Christy resting his eyes during a cease-fire, Kamina, September 1961

weapons and fall in. No one said a word, but you could feel the tension in the air.

Once outside, we could see that this was the largest number on parade in a long time. This could only mean that it was something very serious. I wondered what were we in for this time.

The Company CO stepped out in front of us. "Stand easy," he said, and after a pause continued, "You have all heard by now what happened in Jadotville. Well, it looks like they are now coming to try to take Kamina. Air reconnaissance has informed us that there are about twenty trucks full of troops heading in our direction. You are going out to an ambush area prepared by the 34th battalion. Men, they will not take us. Go and show them that this time they will be the ones to surrender." He turned and walked back into the building. As he got to the door a large roar went up, "Yes, Sir. For Jadotville!"

We passed through 'B' Company lines and could see a large force boarding trucks and jeeps. Desi was sitting next to me. "This is going to be the big one, Desi," I said. He just nodded and stayed deep in his own thoughts.

We were transported about a mile from the ambush location and did a normal patrol out in front, in case they were waiting for us. Once more, you could feel the tension amongst all the troops as we slowly and carefully made our way along the dust road. The corporal out in front put his hand up for us to stop. "Oh God, has he seen them?" I thought. It's not that I was frightened, but there was something about this patrol that looked as if it could end badly.

Word came down the line that there were trenches

on both sides of the road and we were to get into them and stay alert for further orders. I was somehow thankful that it was Desi who jumped into one with me. We were there about two hours when we heard a call. "Come up from the trenches and head back to the trucks. We're going back to base."

We learned later that, up in Kilubi, fifty-five men from 'B' Company had been cut off. The road had been blocked, mined and defended by the enemy. Our men were of no further use up there as the power line had been cut on the evening of the 15th. We were without electric power until we could get our own generators working. These generators supplied emergency lighting for the runways and for the airport control tower.

The Swedish helicopters successfully carried out the evacuation of Kilubi, despite the fact that 'B' Company were constantly being sniped on during their first journey. By altering their route each time, the remainder escaped coming under heavy fire. The rear guard of one officer and seven men destroyed all their stores and equipment before taking off. The enemy could not know whether we were evacuating or re-enforcing the garrison, although the evacuation took most of the night to complete. That unit of 'B' Company was very lucky to get out in one piece.

We heard the following day that Captain Charlie Garneau of the Canadian Signals had intercepted frantic radio messages from Bukama that the Gendarmerie (which we thought of as the enemy) was being overrun by the Balubas. Bukama was on the direct route from Jadotville, so they were diverted there. This put paid to any attack on Kamina that night. Everyone was quiet going back in the truck. I'm sure that, like me, they wondered what might have happened if they had come to Kamina.

We hoped that we would now get a full night's sleep. But, on arrival back at base, we were told to keep our gear on and be ready at a moment's notice to go out if the threat materialised again. Everyone was tossing and turning all through the night. Most of us got up early. Lying there, trying to rest in our full kit was a waste of time. So much for a good night's sleep!

The next day, September 20, our platoon assembled in front of the building, with the support section joining us once more. Lieutenant McMahon told us that today we were going to Gun Hill, a high location overlooking the bridge on the Kolwezi Road. It was on the very edge of the jungle beyond the Officers' Mess in Lumwe. Our job was to secure the hill and give protection to Commandant Moynihan and his engineers while they planted mines and blew up the bridge to prevent any sneak attack coming from that direction.

When we got there, things were very quiet, except for the heat and the frustration of having big, brown ants run all over us. Every now and then, a loud grunt would come from one of the lads and you'd know that he had just been bitten.

Commandant Moynihan fired a flare. That was our signal to pack up and head back to our billets. When we got back, the first thing we did was to shower, washing away the red dust and ants, dead and alive. We were so tired that, after our meal, we collapsed onto our beds. No one had the energy to talk.

I guess that I must have dozed off, as I woke up with a jump when I heard cheering coming from the next billet. Within a minute a corporal walked into our room, his face lit up with a big beaming smile. "Lads it's good news. From midnight tonight, a ceasefire has been called, and we're all still here!" Turning, he walked out to give the news to the next room. There was silence for what seemed like ages, as everyone just looked around at each other. Then a cheer started to build up from the other billets until it sounded like a large sports stadium with hundreds of people shouting and screaming. We hugged each other, slapped each other on the back. Uncontrolled joy. We had made it through. I sat on my bed and my thoughts zigzagged back over the events of the past week.

I was seventeen years old and had been stuck in the middle of firefights in a country where we were posted as peacekeepers, not enforcers. We ended up enforcing the peace by using force of arms, and I remember thinking to myself, "What am I doing here. Why I didn't just go to college or get another job?"

Don't get me wrong; I have no regrets. If anything,

Women of Mwene Ditu, 1961

I am glad that I had this experience and that now, finally, I'm able to write about it. We just did what we were trained to do. Nevertheless, no storytelling, no mix of words or music or recalling of memories can touch that sense of self-worth to have been there and alive in that corner of the world at that time. There were many young Irish lads of the same age serving with me, even several as young as sixteen.

When we read the headlines later in the Irish newspapers saying, "Kamina over-run," it was an indication to us that, back home, no one had heard of the 1st Infantry Group. One newspaper showed a photo of the two Saracens destroyed by us on the first attack, but said that it was the 35th Battalion stationed in Elizabethville, and nowhere near Kamina, who had succeeded in doing it.

Who researched the reports? This really hurt the troop's morale. We had not been 'over-run'.

Katanganese soldiers

sixteen

WHY ME?

After the ceasefire announcement, life carried on. We were still a long way from home, and life never seemed to be that simple, for me anyway. On one occasion, a sergeant tried to force me to receive communion after attending a Mass parade. I refused, for reasons that the readers of this book will be well aware, and he ordered two lads to disarm me and escort me to the guardroom.

The guardroom was a small concrete building manned by two Indian NCOs who were on attachment in Kamina. Several hours after putting me in the cell, they walked in and locked the door after them. They grabbed me. At first, I thought they were just going to work me over, but one of them started to drop his pants down and it was then I realised what they were up to – I had been there before. I managed to get to my feet and kicked where it hurt most the one who had his pants down, knocking him to the floor. The other one backed off and at the same time there was loud banging on the door. It was Sergeant Mooney calling for them to open up. Very quickly, the guard jumped up, pulled up his pants, opened the door and forced a smile at the sergeant saying, "He is a very good prisoner," and he walked away (with some difficulty, I was glad to see).

I never bothered to report them, what would be the point? They were officers, but officers or not, there was no way they were going to overpower me to have their way. I was grown up now and able to protect myself, whatever it took.

Some hours after the ceasefire, and against its intention, the Gendarmerie occupied the farm and the lower end of Base Two. Once more, a platoon had to head down there and quickly pushed them back. This, of course, made extra duties, as a platoon then had to stay in this area to prevent any further incursions. A platoon already occupied Gun Hill. Company Headquarters at the EPA also had to be guarded, and there were constant patrols moving around the perimeter to make sure that there wasn't any movement of Katanganese army troops, who might have been trying to take advantage of the ceasefire.

From September 21 onwards, we still had to man our outer defences and hold the ground we had won. Still no break from twenty-four hours on and twenty-four hours off. The duties were overwhelming.

There are always rumours when groups of soldiers are together. From October 2, the camp chat was all about where we could be posted next. Many thought that we might be moved to Elizabethville to join up with the 35th Battalion. Everyone hoped that this one was true. Having been in the Congo jungle living in tents for four months, being stationed in a modern town would have been really great news.

Later that day, word was passed down to pack up our kit and belongings and to be ready, as there was an imminent move about to take place to an unspecified location. On hearing that, fears of another posting in the jungle were rife. Could they do this to us again?

Eventually, it was October 9 when we received word. With less than twenty-four hours' notice, we were told that we would be moved to Niemba. This destination was later expanded upon, and on Tuesday October 10, advanced elements from our 'B' Company reached Nyunzu. The Swedish company that had been with us since our arrival in Kamina, joined us there. So, once more, our group took over from a Ghanaian battalion and reconnaissance squadron.

Unfortunately, we were delayed until the Thursday due to mechanical breakdowns and the non-arrival of the scheduled planes. This made life very difficult as we had already handed in our 'non-essential' personal belongings to be stored in Kamina Base until we were due to return home.

Finally, the planes did arrive, and, on landing in Albertville, one of the other platoons marched straight to a DC-2 plane waiting at the airport, but we had to wait for trucks to transport us to the railway station. As we were still in the Congo, the train had, as usual broken down. We were informed that we would be staying at the station overnight. No arrangements had been made for this unplanned delay, so we just had to poke out a place to rest and try to get some sleep. I was standing there wondering what to do, when I heard Desi's voice call out, "Christy, Christy, over here!"

I felt as if I was in a dream (maybe it was the heat or just that I was pissed off heading back into the jungle), but I couldn't see him. Then I heard Joey's voice using one of his favourite phrases, "Come on, ya dope, we're over here, in the carriage on your right."

I spotted the two of them with their heads stuck out of a train carriage window, big smiles on their faces. As I walked over, my mind suddenly went back to twelve months ago and my adventures on the train tracks to Dublin. God, that felt like another life, and a lifetime ago since I had to sleep in a carriage in the station there. Why does life throw up such reminders of things that you just want to forget? "Will you come on, or we'll give your seat to someone else!" they both roared. This brought me back to reality and I ran over to join them.

All we had to eat was the little bags of food we had been given as a light snack to get us over the 'short journey', consisting of some hard biscuits and fruit.

Our train finally pulled into the station at 08.00 hours on the morning of October 13, and we boarded, heading off to our new posting in Northern Katanga. For a change, this was a pleasant and rapid journey, and the scenery flew by. It looked almost like back home, with green hills and woods – just like passing through Wicklow. After five hours, we arrived in Nyunzu. It felt that this might be a better posting. How wrong we were.

Again, as in South Kasai, we were the first white troops to fully occupy these areas. Once more, into the bush, and again into tents, this time at the height of the rainy season. There were times when we worked and slept in wet clothes. These conditions were a real nightmare when the rain would come in sudden deluges and saturate the soil. It would transform the ground into red-coloured clay, which would get into our clothes and skin. It was hot by day and cold by night.

Our mission in Nyunzu was to guard the airstrip, which was a ribbon of land hacked out of the jungle, just long enough for a small plane to land. Other duties included protecting the approach to the town from Niemba. We also had one hundred and forty-four Katangese Gendarmerie prisoners to look after, in addition to guarding the town, a railway and a main road network. Again, we found ourselves among the Balubas. We did frequent patrols to Niemba, and 'B' Company organised a pilgrimage to the scene of last November's ambush. We hoped to erect a permanent memorial on the site before we left.

Our group of about three hundred and fifty soldiers, including the Swedish company, had once more taken over a location previously manned by a Ghanaian battalion and reconnaissance squadron. We were now doing the duties and work that had taken about one thousand soldiers to do before us This burden was taking its toll on all of us.

Another event that nearly escalated into something very serious happened on October 29, when five hundred of Tshombe's troops attempted to enter the town through the Kongolo barrier, to set up a garrison there. Lieutenant Colonel O'Donovan, the Group CO, put us on alert, ready to use force, and our presence drove them away.

The next day about one hundred of them arrived back with the intention of setting up a smaller outpost. Once more, Colonel O'Donovan wasn't having it. He advised them that he would use force to remove them. I'm sure it was because of what had happened at Kamina and other locations when they had gone into battle against the Irish that gave them a good enough reason to back down.

With the exception of sixteen days in Kamina, we had continuously been at 'battle stations' for many months. Morale, which was very high when things were toughest, had been dropping steadily with the arrival of each batch of newspapers from Ireland. Once again, we realised that our group did not exist in the minds of the Irish public. Kamina was thought of as an outpost of the 35th battalion in Elizabethville. But Kamina is over 200 miles from Elizabethville, and was an independent command, but this seemed to be lost on the media. While we didn't seek recognition, it was demoralising to see our efforts not given credit in any way.

This group had always been a tight unit. We were battle trained and seasoned troops before the battle of Katanga. We stood up well to each hardship that was thrown at us. We were sent to the worst, most isolated and troubled areas of the Congo. And, despite the filthy, miserable conditions, we survived. The men of the First Infantry Group did an excellent job, considering the hardships they had endured during their tour, but General Headquarters seemed to be unaware of our record.

During our entire tour, we were never stationed near a town with shops or modern amenities. We spent most of our service in the Congo posted to small, primitive towns, where we were confined to our camps because all of those areas were trouble spots.

Between 1960 and 1964, a total of eight Irish battalions and two infantry groups served in the Congo, including two armoured car units and many personnel on UN Headquarters staff. Twenty-six Irish soldiers lost their lives and fifty-seven were injured.

'B' Company placing a cross at the site of the Niemba ambush where nine Irish UN soldiers lost their lives, August 1961

Bren gun bunker, Nyunzu, August 1961

I found it very strange that, even though the UN were involved in the planning of combat action, and apart from our first briefing back home, it was never explained to us who we were fighting and why, or the reasons why we, as peacekeepers, were defending ourselves from attacks by government troops. We never fully knew the political side of the Congo, or if we had done any real good out there, but we always did our duty to the best of our ability.

Any bad situations I got myself into in the Congo and any incidents I have written about were my own fault. As a seventeen-year-old teenager I did some stupid things, sometimes nearly causing the loss of my own life, purely through clumsiness.

My story could be similar to the stories of many of those men who served alongside me – incidents that our officers and headquarters knew nothing about, incidents that were never recorded. So many stories of bravery, comradeship, hardship and even fun have gone unreported and undocumented. So many veterans from the Congo have already passed away and their stories are lost.

I have been called a hero many times by my fellow veterans, and all I can say is that if I am a hero, then it was by accident. I never think of myself as a hero. I consider myself a survivor, just like I was a survivor from Greenmount and Upton Industrial schools as a child.

I made it home in one piece.

Making sandwiches. Fresh bread was a rare treat – dog biscuits were the norm

Troops in a truck. Both pics, 1961

seventeen

HOME

When the 1st Infantry Group returned from the Congo, we were taken to our separate home units. I was brought to Cathal Brugha Barracks in Dublin, where I was allowed to start my four weeks leave. I got a bus to the Bank of Ireland in the centre of the city, still in my uniform, and made my way to Townsend Street. I can remember the feeling of walking through my neighbourhood and being greeted by several of my neighbours before I reached Markievicz Flats. It was the most amazing feeling ever. I was so proud, and also grateful that I made it home alive.

Perhaps I had sometimes been a bit careless or naive, or even too keen to prove to myself that I was the perfect soldier. I had spent so many years prior to joining the army, being intimidated, bullied and made to believe that I was worthless and that I would never amount to anything. The Congo proved that all those demeaning words were totally wrong. In those six months I had proved my worth in the cause of peace.

I went to the Congo as a boy and returned as a man. I never did another tour with the United Nations, but, after that powerful experience things were never really the same again.

When I got home to our one bedroom flat on the

The bridge to Jadotville from Kamina airbase, 1961

Liam O'Leary (Kanturk) and Dan 'Scan' Buckley (Cork), Mwene Ditu, 1961

third floor, I found my mam ill in her bed. I called for an ambulance and she was rushed to the hospital. I spent my four weeks leave going back and forth between home and the hospital, and didn't report back for duty for a further week until I knew she was going to be okay.

On my return to Cathal Brugha Barracks, I was taken into custody and brought before my commanding officer the following morning to be charged with being absent without official leave (AWOL).

He was understanding regarding Mam's health and only confined me to barracks for a week. I found it very strange mixing with other soldiers who didn't know who the 1st Infantry group was. "Never heard of them," was their reaction. They kept asking, "Yes, but which battalion were you with?" and "Where were you in the Congo?" Even the NCOs never heard of the 1st infantry group.

I later learned that many of my fellow soldiers experienced the same reaction, and it was frustrating to say the least. All my army friends say they heard about the Battle of Jadotville and the Battle of the Tunnel, but had never heard of the of the fighting in Kamina.

For the next few months, I suffered from migraine, and no amount of painkillers worked. The only way to relieve the pain was to lie down in the dark for a few hours.

I found it hard to settle down. My Commanding Officer thought that it might be good for me to take a driving course. A few lessons in, while returning to barracks at the end of a session, the instructor, seated in the passenger seat, was being aggressive, and I was trying to pay attention to him. I took my eye off the entrance and hit the gates. I was removed from the course.

In 1963, during the visit of President John F. Kennedy, I was selected to be part of the Guard of Honour at Leinster House for Éamon de Valera, the President of Ireland, and accompanied him while he inspected the troops.

The first time I had ever seen President was when I was eight years old, and he was Taoiseach. My mam had worked at the government buildings and cleaned his office twice daily, also serving him his tea and biscuits. She worked there for over twenty years and Mr. de Valera knew her very well. Saturday was her half-day, and every second Saturday I would meet her outside the church in Westland Row and we would go to the local cinema. It was my treat and I always looked forward to it.

On one particular Saturday, Mr. de Valera was walking along Westland Row in his smart black overcoat and hat, carrying an umbrella. He noticed Mam and approached us.

"Hello Martha, and is this your little boy?" She grabbed me and pushed me behind her to prevent him from seeing the patches on the back of my trousers. She made small talk with him for a couple of minutes, telling him that she was taking me to the cinema. He reached into his pocket and, taking out a small purse, handed me a threepenny bit, patting me on the head saying, "Buy some sweets young man, and enjoy the cinema." I looked up at him and knew he was a very important man. My mam pinched my arm and said, "Where's your manners? Thank the nice man, Christy." I did, and he waved his hat, going on his way with a smile on his face. When Mam told me who he was, I think I told everybody in the flats that I met de Valera and that he gave me a threepenny bit. I thought I was rich, having so much money, and bought three bars of toffee at the cinema.

And so I was looking forward to being part of the Guard of Honour and seeing President de Valera again and, of course, President Kennedy. I spent the whole night cleaning my boots and equipment and pressing my trousers.

The next day, as they inspected our Guard of Honour, de Valera paused in front of me for a couple of seconds. When the inspection was complete, my sergeant approached me and informed me I was on a charge for untidiness while on parade. I questioned him why, and went a little too far when I gave him a mouthful. I ended up being taken to the guardroom when we got back to barracks.

I was brought before my Commanding Officer the following morning, fined £3, and confined to barracks for seven days. All this just because the President paused in front of me during the inspection. It was a known fact that he was short-sighted, and I feel to this day that he was only trying to figure out where he knew me from.

I was glad that I got to see JFK face to face. Not long after his very successful visit to Ireland, this very popular president was assassinated in Dallas.

I performed guard duties at Cathal Brugha Barracks,

Clancy Barracks and Government Buildings on Merrion Street. On one occasion while on guard duty at Government Buildings, I was approached by a young corporal who was also stationed there. He made a point of letting me know he knew Mam very well from working with her there. He didn't seem to be afraid to tell me he was involved with the IRA and tried to recruit me.

One of the places he was interested in was Clancy Barracks, where arms and ammunition were stored. He suggested that I might be able to assist them, knowing that I did guard duties there. He was blunt about it and had no fear of me reporting him. This made me very nervous. I turned him down very politely and again he reminded me that he knew my mam. I took that as a warning to keep my mouth shut, and to this day I have. Mam was pleased when I told her that I had met her friend while on guard duty and all she could say was that he was a very nice man.

The migraines were growing in severity, and there were times when I even lost consciousness. My friends told me that my body would shake wildly each time I passed out, and that I acted strangely when I woke up. This scared them. I hadn't a clue what was happening me.

It was around this time I went on a cooking course at Clancy Barracks. I enjoyed it and managed to hide my illness for months. That is, until I was sent to Gormanston Camp for two weeks to cook for one hundred and fifty FCA personnel from the reserve units. Once more I began to have violent seizures. When I returned to the NCO's mess to cook in Cathal Brugha Barracks, my fits were observed by one of the sergeants.

He reported me, and I was sent to Saint Bricin's army hospital. The seizures got worse and more frequent. On one occasion, I was told that I was violent when I woke up, and had fought off the soldiers who were holding me down. Ever since my days in Upton, I hated to be restrained in any way, even in horseplay, so I always react badly in these situations.

It got so bad that I was put in a room guarded by two soldiers twenty-four hours a day. I was never told by the army doctors what was happening to me, and treatment wasn't forthcoming. One of the soldiers told me that I was possessed by something evil and he was instructed to use whatever force necessary to keep me in that hospital room. The army doctors hadn't a clue, so they proposed to have me sent to St Brendan's hospital for the mentally ill. If there was one thing I was sure of, it was that I wasn't mentally ill, and I refused to allow them to send me there.

At no time did they give me any treatment, tests or explanations. They didn't know what was wrong with me, and I also didn't understand what was going on in my head. I was quite clear that, outside these attacks, I was very much in my right mind. But the army decided that if I refused to go to a mental hospital, they would have to discharge me on medical grounds.

In April 1965, I was discharged, and my papers stated, "Below physical standard." This was untrue. I was physically fit, spending a lot of my time in the gym. If the papers had said, "Below medical standard," I would have been able to apply for a disability pension. They contacted my mam to collect me. After five years in the army I was now a civilian.

Being discharged was hurtful and depressing

because I had served my country and the world in general by serving with the UN in the Congo. Over there I did my duty as ordered, and, without complaining, had put my life on the line to protect others. Did they not check my medical records and notice that I had been in hospital for a head injury? It was so easy for them to throw me on the scrap-heap without a thought. After all I had experienced as a soldier, good and bad, I was heartbroken. I had always believed I would remain in the army until retirement.

But, once the army had decided on my dismissal, there was little point in arguing. It's a well-known fact that if a soldier has seizures, they are not fit for duty. Why the seizures happened was irrelevant. No one cared enough to enquire, and I had no idea there could possibly be medical reasons for them, let alone a treatment that could manage them.

Around this time, I was dating my girlfriend, Mary, and she supported me, despite witnessing my seizures. She came from Fethard in County Tipperary and worked in Dublin, where she stayed with her uncle, Bill Casey. She once told me that she suspected I was an epileptic, but I suppose I was in denial.

I made many attempts to find work in Dublin and attended several interviews, only to be turned down. It is hard to get a job when a would-be employer knows you were discharged from the army on medical grounds, especially when you are asked what those medical grounds were. I didn't accept at that time that my seizures were indeed caused by epilepsy. I believed that no business would employ someone who could have seizures at any time of the day or night.

Christy and Mary, London, 1965

eighteen

LONDON

I met up with my friend Desi Jordan who had served with me in the Congo. He had left the army. We both had a problem finding work and decided to travel to London. He was very aware of my seizures and it was a blessing to have him travelling with me. We both went to Chelsea Barracks and asked to sign up for the British army. I really thought that I could resume my army career.

Desi failed the writing test, but I was lucky to pass by the skin of my teeth. Just as the recruiting sergeant was arranging my warrant to travel to the North of Ireland, all hell broke loose. I went into a grand mal seizure and scared the hell out of him. It must have been the shock of being sent to the North of Ireland. They called an ambulance and I ended up spending the next week in a hospital having test after test. I didn't wait for the results, as I was afraid that if I admitted to myself that I had epilepsy, I would never have got a job.

The army life was not to be, and I had to accept it and move on as best I could in the UK, a strange country that I knew absolutely nothing about. It was a bit of a shock for Desi and myself when we tried to find accommodation.

Everywhere we looked in London, we were turned away. Signs everywhere said, 'No Irish, No Blacks and No Animals'. In Shepherd's Bush we found a room to let in an Irish middle-aged couple's house. We couldn't wait to settle down for the night, we were so exhausted from walking around London. At 5.30 the following morning our new Irish landlord was banging on our room door and shouting, "Get up and find work!"

Desi and I took his advice and cleared out of the house very quickly and never returned. Getting kicked out of our lodgings at 5.30 every morning is not something either of us could tolerate, so we decided to try to find live-in employment in one of the London hotels. We got a job in the Royal Hotel in Russell Square as porters, and also managed to arrange a job there for Mary, so we could carry on seeing each other.

She arrived three weeks later and we remained working in the hotel for the next eight months. The frequency of the seizures lessened with the help of medication. This was prescribed after I had been out one evening with Mary and some friends. One of them kept buying me whiskey and I drank too much. That same evening I had a seizure and Mary called an ambulance, and the duty doctor suspected epilepsy and prescribed the medication. I was still in denial, but decided to take the medication until it ran out.

At this time, I wasn't registered with a GP, so when it ran out I continued to have frequent seizures and Mary dealt with them on her own, making me comfortable and safe. Not a great excuse, but to be honest I always knew if I was registered as an epileptic my chances of finding work with a proper wage were limited. Hence my silence about my condition and keeping my current job.

Furthermore, I came to recognise the warning signs when I was about to have one. I found this very helpful because it enabled me to hide my condition from my employer.

When we got our first pay packet, Desi and I went into Piccadilly Circus and fell for the three-card trick, losing all our wages. You live and learn, eh?

Desi wasn't too happy working in the hotel, and he asked me to join him working on the construction sites of the new Victoria Tube line. The job was digging underground and getting the soil up to the surface. On piecework, the money was more than double what we earned in the hotel.

It was hard work, spending twelve hour shifts in compressed air over one hundred and seventy feet below the ground. There was no room for wasters who would put extra work on everyone else in a work-gang, but thankfully, they were usually spotted quickly and let go.

Mary and I got married in a registry office on November 12 1966, on a very cold day, but the warmth in our hearts made up for that. She was very understanding about how I felt regarding the Catholic Church and was quite happy about getting married in a registry office. We were very much in love.

Losing my job wasn't new to me. If I had a seizure during work I was either sacked or I walked. Each time I lost my job I would make my way to another tunnel site and be employed within days. I had to keep working because Mary was now expecting our first child. Signing on the dole was never an option I favoured. I was told that I could claim disability allowance due to my epilepsy and wouldn't have to work. But I remained working until Mary was near the end of her pregnancy.

I couldn't believe it when we discovered she was carrying twin boys and, although a month premature, they were healthy and beautiful. We named them Robert and Christopher. Because we now had babies, we were asked to leave our rented accommodation, a one-bedroom flat on the third floor of a block. The landlord had a 'no children' policy. We were given one month's notice. Finding another flat was a nightmare.

A week before we had to vacate, we got lucky and found a landlord who normally let out his flat to a family with one child. However, he agreed to let us move in, saying he would make an exception for twins. It was an upstairs flat in Hornsey, North London.

After a couple of months, we had a complaint from the couple downstairs about the thumping noise. I explained that it was just my twins trying to stand up, but sometimes falling down on their bottoms. But the complaints about any kind of noise carried on for several weeks and got to the point where we were even afraid to turn on our TV.

The man downstairs was a very tall, well-built man who looked like he spent a lot of his time in the gym. I needed to be careful not to give him any excuse to turn violent and end up getting evicted for fighting.

It all came to a head one evening while I was using a saw to cut the corners off a square table because I was afraid the twins might bang their heads on them when trying to climb. The man came to our door, repeatedly banging on it and shouting abuse. I knew I had to open the door and explain what I was doing with the saw. I was a little angry and I ran to open the door, waving my arms in the air, only I forgot to put the saw down before I opened the door. All this man could see was his angry, noisy neighbour swinging his arms and threatening him with a saw. He backed off and ran down the stairs shouting to his wife to call the police.

I started to follow him down the stairs to try and explain that I wasn't going to attack him, but he locked himself into his flat. When I realised he wasn't in a listening mood, it was then that I noticed the saw was still in my hand. A couple of minutes later the police arrived and I explained everything that happened, assuring them that I had no intention of attacking him.

After listening to both sides, they came up to our flat to see what I was doing with the saw. They were satisfied with my explanation and they stayed with us for a while, fascinated by my identical twin boys.

My landlord was informed of the incident by the guy downstairs, and he asked us to leave, giving us a month's notice. In addition to facing eviction, I was also sacked from my current job as a binman because I'd had a seizure the previous day. Under the Health and Safety Act, they couldn't have an epileptic working on a HGV bin lorry. We refused to leave the flat and the landlord started proceedings against us. But, before the case was due to come up, for reasons that were never explained, it was postponed.

By now, Mary was pregnant with our third child and we were desperate to find somewhere else to live. It was going to be very difficult to find a landlord who would accept a family with three children. We were very much alone, as we didn't have any family living in the UK that could have helped us. I found a flat in Turnpike Lane, North London and told the landlord we had no kids, and that it was just just Mary and I. We were desperate, and decided if we found a flat where the landlord wasn't resident, then we could hide the kids. How stupid was that? We got away with it as long as we paid the rent and kept a low profile.

I worked on many building sites, but each time I either got the sack or walked off the job due to my seizures. It was easier to get another job if you left a job, rather than being sacked.

My GP was concerned at the frequency of the seizures and increased the dosage of my medication. In the weeks that followed I could feel the improvement. They became less frequent, and that helped me to hold down jobs for longer.

I found out that there was more work available on the Tube line construction, and that they were offering great money, so I made my way to the site at King's Cross. It was too late, all labouring posts were filled, but there was a vacancy for a crane driver. I lied to the foreman that I had been a crane driver in Ireland and asked him for the job. I was told to report to the site the next morning at 6.

The next day, before starting, I spent a good hour checking out and testing the controls. It was very basic, with just two handles for up and down along with a foot pedal. When the lads who were digging needed materials sent down the one-hundred-foot shaft, my job was to lower that material down to them. I couldn't see the bottom of the shaft from the cab of the crane, so there was always a man standing at the top of the shaft giving me signals. The job went very well for the next four months and I was earning a good wage. But the guy who was giving me directions went sick one week and had to be replaced.

On the new guy's first day, I noticed he was a little slack in giving me directions when I was lowering material down the shaft and had to warn him there could be an accident if he gave me the wrong hand signals. Another day I noticed that he was more interested in reading a newspaper than giving me directions. I really couldn't trust him.

On a very quiet night shift, when there was not a lot to be done, I decided that I had to do something to cover myself from any accidents before I started back on day shift.

I lowered the crane cable down to the bottom of the shaft very slowly and once I was satisfied it was at the bottom, I tied a red rag onto the cable at my end. This way, I would be able to tell how close I was to the bottom of the shaft, so when the cable was only a foot from the end, I would slow down the rate of descent and lower it gently the rest of the way.

This worked perfectly for me for several days and, although the signalman was giving me instructions, I was happy that, even if he made a bad signal, I was always able to see the red rag tied to my cable that indicated I was nearly at the bottom. Occasionally I had to lower workmen down the shaft. They would step into a large metal bucket connected to the crane cable. I would then lower them down and, when the red rag came into view, I knew that they were almost at their destination.

One day I was told by the foreman that two London Transport Officers were coming to inspect the tunnel and I would have to lower them down to the bottom of the shaft with 'due care'. They arrived at 1pm, both dressed in smart suits and ties. My foreman helped them into the metal bucket and the signalman attached the crane cable hook onto it. So, I had two important men and my foreman to lower down the shaft. I proceeded to lower them down as carefully as I could, while keeping an eye out for that red rag to appear.

The cable went down and down and the red rag just didn't appear. I felt a hard jolt and a loud bang so I stopped the crane. The red rag had disappeared off the cable and the signalman had not given me any direction that they were almost at the bottom. The metal bucket with the three men inside had hit the ground hard. This could have caused very serious injuries. I jumped out of the crane and looked down. I could see the cable loosely wrapped around the men. Somehow, they managed to get out of the bucket, dusted themselves down, smoothed their jackets, straightened their ties and thankfully, walked away without any injuries.

I shouted down, "You guys all right?" My foreman screamed back that they were OK and then roared loudly and angrily, "Fleming, pick up your fucking cards."

I swear that signal guy removed my red rag because I had complained about him. But, if he did, he hadn't done himself any favours because he was also fired.

Mary was close to her time for our third child, so finding another job was my priority. I applied for a job with London Transport and, after an interview and a medical, I was offered a job as a bus conductor.

It was 1967 when our child was born, a beautiful girl we named Alice. Somehow, our landlord found out that we had three children and he wasn't too pleased that I had lied to him. He wanted us out and gave us a month's notice.

Mary found an advertisement in the newspaper where a landlord was looking for a live-in housekeeper to look after twenty flats in Bayswater. The job included collecting rents and supervising three cleaners. She was offered the job, and the owner was happy with our twin boys as long as it didn't interfere with her work. She failed to tell him that we also had a baby girl. The job was just what we needed. We were given the basement flat and Mary was paid a wage.

At last, things were looking up for us. We were both earning, and living in a flat with our three children. If the landlord called, we would hide our little girl.

I had started my bus career on the No 73 – a very long route – which ran from Stoke Newington, through the West End of London, Oxford Street, Hyde Park, Chelsea and on to Richmond.

On my first shift, which was late at night, there were drunks jumping on and off, some without paying. At one stage, three Irish lads who were pissed out of their minds jumped on and took over the long seat, stretching out their legs, preventing me from passing to collect fares. They were young lads like myself but, when I asked them to let me pass, I was told to fuck off. In an angry voice, one of them also replied, "Go and fuck yourself, fucking English bastard."

I wanted so much to tell them I was a true 'Dub' of pure Irish blood, but I thought better of it and decided not to engage with them, as they were looking for a fight. I stepped over their outstretched long legs and continued to collect fares from passengers. I knew I would eventually have to approach them and ask for their fares. As I was heading back to confront them, the three of them jumped off, without having paid their fares, as the bus was slowing down. In a way, I was not too bothered and just got on with my job. I checked the long seat they occupied and noticed a crumpled-up envelope. I opened it, and there were two fivers and three one-pound notes inside, a total of £13. It must have slipped out of one of their back pockets, and looked like a pay packet.

Okay, now you're wondering what I did with the money – did I hand it in or pocket it? I'm afraid I kept it and I didn't feel that I was being dishonest, because I believed that, after their terrible behaviour they deserved to lose the money. However, just to be safe, I checked at the depot at the end of my shift just to see if any one of them had rung in asking if their money was found. If they had, I would have handed it in.

You might ask why I didn't do the honest thing and hand it in anyway. Well, it's like this, anybody that calls me out to fight, I can deal with, but anyone who calls me names makes me choke. I felt no guilt whatsoever in keeping their money.

However, when I got home and told Mary what had happened, she got very angry and insisted that I hand it in. On my next shift, I gave it to my supervisor.

The early Saturday shifts on the 73 buses were particularly busy due to the number of tourists. They were full of questions about where was this place and that. If you know the West End of London, then you will understand that, even back in 1967, traffic travelled at only about ten miles per hour, stopping and starting. It took ages to travel the length of Oxford Street. I was continuously giving directions to tourists and at times, I was able to jump off to show them directions to, for example, Bond Street and jump back on before my bus started to move in the crawling traffic.

One particular Saturday, a couple of lovely Americans were struggling to understand the directions I was giving them in my Irish accent, so, as the bus was crawling along Oxford Street, I jumped off with them to direct them to one of the theatres. By the time I managed to put them straight, my bus had started to move away, and I had to run like mad to get back on and unusually, it was really going fast. I was lucky that I managed to scramble on board. I immediately proceeded to collect fares on the bottom deck and once I finished there I made my way to the upper deck and called out, "Fares please, thank you." Halfway along the upper deck a guy in uniform shouted, "Hey you, get off my bus!" I paused and then shouted back at him, "You're on the wrong bus, this is the 73." He walked over and whispered in my ear, to make sure the passengers couldn't hear, "This is the 25, you twat, now get off my bus!"

So now I am a bus conductor walking along Oxford Street without a bus, and the 73, which was at this stage most likely somewhere around Knightsbridge, was without a conductor. I thought I might be able to save my dignity by jumping on another bus that went the same way, but that didn't work out, as my driver had had already reported what had happened. The passengers had been shouting at him that there was no one to give them their tickets. I had neglected my responsibility for the safety of members of the public who used the bus service, and London Transport was very strict about that. I was once again out of work.

The next day I picked up my insurance cards and headed once again to the Labour Exchange, looking for a new job.

Once more Lady Luck smiled on us. Our landlord asked me if I could decorate all the twelve flats in the building at a rate of £150 per flat. Although I never did decorating in my life, I was happy to have a go at it and, for a novice, didn't do too badly. After successfully finishing the first sixteen within a couple of months, he surprised me by paying in advance for the last four flats. This was a morale boost for me, because it showed that he had come to trust me.

Mary had a small problem with one of the three cleaners. She was never on time and neglected many of her cleaning duties. Mary warned her that she could lose her job if she continued in this way.

The residents were complaining about this woman's poor standards of cleaning, so Mary had no choice but to give her a final warning. She told Mary to stuff her job and left in a very angry state. Then she proved her character by contacting the owner and told him that we had three children and not two, one being a baby girl. He was very upset and complained that we had taken advantage of him. He had no mercy. He told us that we had to be off the premises by the time he got back from holiday, in a couple of weeks.

Once more our luck had changed for the worse. We both got into a state because we knew that finding another flat with three children within two weeks wasn't going to happen. We visited the Council, asking if they could help us to find accommodation. The best they could offer was to take Mary and the children into Council care, and that I would have to fend for myself. We didn't want to be separated, but we were told that if we refused, Social Services would take our children into care anyway.

We didn't take long to make the decision to go back home to Ireland. Hopefully our families would be able to help us. No time was wasted, and we travelled on the ferry that very night, buying tickets with the last of our money.

HOME AGAIN

Mary and the kids stayed with her parents in Tipperary while I moved in with my mother in Dublin, intending to look for work. It was difficult for both of us, but I made a point of spending every weekend with them in Tipperary. But I needed to get a job soon, and although my mother helped me with fares when visiting them, we couldn't carry on with this arrangement indefinitely.

Early one morning, I walked to the Dublin docks, where every day there was a queue of men hoping to get a day's work unloading the cargo ships. I, along with another three blokes, failed to get picked but returned the next morning. Once again, I failed to get selected and turned to made my way back home. As the three of us were walking away, a van pulled in and the driver shouted out, "Can any one of ye drive a lorry?" I waited for one of the guys to answer and they just nodded their heads, saying nothing. I knew I was taking one hell of a risk, but it seems most of my life I had been doing that, so I told him that I was a driver. "Jump in, I have a delivery that needs to go today."

He took me to a large garage, handed me a bunch of keys and said, "Take this lorry carrying ten tons of cement to Bray." I was handed keys without even being asked to show my driving licence. Which was just as well, as I didn't have one. I was given a helper, which was also just as well because I wasn't sure if I could remember the way to Bray.

We got back late that evening after unloading the cement, and the garage was closed. I drove the lorry back to Markievicz Flats and parked it up. I returned to the depot early the following morning and the foreman was quite happy for me to keep it overnight, as long as I turned up with it the following day. For a couple of weeks, I was driving all over the city, earning good money.

One day, I collected large boxes of tea from one of the ships along the docks. It was my job to have them cleared through Customs and then transport them to their destination. It was lunchtime by the time they were free of Customs. So, being quite close to home, I decided to have lunch with Mam. There was no point going on with the delivery as the consignee was closed for lunch.

During that break I had a seizure and my mother called an ambulance. I ended up in hospital for several hours and during that time my foreman came knocking on her door looking for the keys of the lorry that was parked up outside. So that was the end of my new job.

My medical condition was an obstruction to my everyday life, as was the pain and poor vision in my left eye. I was unable to hold down any job, and I was missing Mary and the kids terribly. I was terrified that they would forget their dad. I wanted so much to be there for them. They needed a father. I had been brought up without a father and I didn't want that for my children.

During a weekend in Tipperary, I suggested to Mary that I should return to London where there was lots of work. It wasn't an easy decision, but if I was to get all my family back together again, it could only happen in London. She gave me her blessing and it was agreed that I would go, find work and a flat, and they would follow me as soon as possible. This had to happen. I just couldn't bear the thought of us being apart for long periods. It was breaking my heart.

I contacted my friend Desi, and he was able to let me share the room he rented in Highbury, North London. Over the next couple of months, I worked on three separate sites and got sacked from all of them because I had seizures.

It became apparent I wasn't fit to work on building sites, which would have been my main avenue of employment. I began to feel very depressed, but I couldn't register for any treatment with a GP during those few months, as I didn't have a proper home address, being put up by various friends.

Every day I checked the newspapers for jobs, and, one day, spotted a vacancy for a packer. Unfortunately, the job was quite a distance away. I didn't have the fare, and on the spur of the moment and in total desperation, I picked the lock of the gas meter. I took out my return fare of six shillings, with the intention of returning it when I could. I felt like I was committing a bank robbery. It wasn't my style and I hated myself. I got the job and got through the first day without having a seizure.

When I got back to the lodgings there was a lot of fuss going on between my friend Desi and the landlady. It seems I forgot to re-secure the meter lock when I borrowed the money. I had to come clean, as she had been accusing Desi. She wasn't very forgiving and called the police to report the theft. She also made a point of telling them that I was not one of her lodgers.

I ended up at the police station giving a statement to explain how I got myself in this mess. Just when I thought it couldn't get any worse, the police informed me that they had discovered there was a warrant out for my arrest. It seems that when Mary and I left the block of flats in London, we should have returned the advance money the owner had paid me for the decorating work, and he reported it to the police. He told them that I had taken £450 from the premises and disappeared. They classified it as a crime. I couldn't argue with them. The more I thought about it, the more I realised we did actually steal that money, as I had never finished the decorating work. I was charged for theft of that amount, and for stealing six shillings from the meter.

Because I had no fixed abode, I was kept in a cell until the following morning, from where I was taken to court. At the hearing, I was assigned a probation officer who would look into my circumstances and file a report on me to the magistrate. I was remanded for two weeks awaiting further reports and taken to Brixton Prison. The probation officer, without my knowledge, contacted Mary in Tipperary and told her what had happened.

I had three seizures during the two weeks in Brixton and they had me on suicide watch. After a week, Mary turned up to visit me. She was staying with the kids at a house which had been arranged by the probation officer. He felt that it would be in my favour to have Mary and the kids back in London. Seeing them raised my spirits, which were at a very low ebb.

On the day of my court appearence, I was expecting to be sent back to prison, and it was the worst feeling ever. One of the saddest moments of my life was seeing the fear in Mary's eyes. As she cuddled the children close to her, tears rolled down her face and by this time I couldn't hold them back either as I walked into the dock. When would we hold each other again? What had we done wrong in our lives to deserve this? Had I not been punished enough throughout my life so far? Poor Mary.

The magistrate took into account my epilepsy, and put me on twelve months' probation and I was allowed to leave the court with my wife and children.

twenty

REDBRIDGE

Our accomodation in London was only temporary, and we were under pressure to find somewhere more permanent. One of the people living there suggested I contact a group who were helping families to squat in properties in the London Borough of Redbridge.

Redbridge Council had been buying up properties to make way for the construction of a ring road that wouldn't be completed for ten years. They had bought these buildings and planned to leave them empty during the first stage of development. They were due to stay that way and then be demolished at the commencement of the second stage of construction.

The squatting campaign members had already taken over a house in Ilford, and had prepared it for us to move in. I then had to inform the Council that I had moved in and offer to pay rent on the understanding that I would vacate when they began the second phase of the ring road. I also let them know that I had every intention of finding a flat as soon as my circumstances changed. They refused my offer and applied to the courts to have us evicted.

They also pointed out that, as soon as I became homeless, it was more than likely that the Council would have to take my children into care. It wasn't a perfect situation for my family to be in. Squatting was a new world to us and I felt guilty involving my family in such an perilous arrangement.

There were several homeless families being helped by the squatters association, and the Council felt under pressure to act urgently and put a stop to the occupations. So, they decided to act illegally and hired a gang of neo-fascist thugs under the command of Barrie Quartermain, a friend of Mosley of the National Front movement. The bullying methods of Quartermain were also used for strike-breaking.

During March and April 1969, the Council's mercenaries made violent raids on three of the Ilford houses, evicting the occupants and making those families homeless. On two occasions in June, they made further attacks on two more houses. Although they were wearing helmets, carrying shields and equipped with bricks to throw at the windows, they were beaten back by residents and forced to give up.

This defeat was bad news for my family, when the time came to try to evict us, Quatermain had increased the size of his 'army' to as many as fifty thugs. It was 5.30 on a Wednesday morning when the front door was broken down. They charged in and started to smash the hall furniture and the banisters of the staircase. Mary and I were asleep in the same room as the three children, as we never wanted to let them out of our sight. We had been expecting this day.

I heard the loud footsteps of men running up the stairs and jumped out of my bed to stand by the children's bed to protect them. I was aware of what these thugs were capable of and I expected them to be violent. The first guy to burst open our bedroom door was called The Seven-Foot Wanderer, as he was the first one to appear at every eviction around London – probably the biggest thug of them all.

I spread my arms in front of the children's bed to protect them, but by now the room was full of these scumbags, shouting at us to get out. The Seven-Foot Wanderer punched me in the stomach and then pulled two of my kids from the bed. I managed to push him back and grabbed the twins whilst Mary carried our two-year-old girl. We were bundled out of the flat. The children were screaming. It was difficult carrying the twins, one in each arm, down the stairs, especially when there were now no banisters, while the thugs were manhandling us. By now the house was almost completely wrecked and, within a few days, it had been knocked down and turned into a car park for the Council.

Social services were standing outside waiting for my family to come out and to take my children into care. They could only do this if we were homeless, as there were no other grounds, because my children were well looked after and there was no neglect. I refused to hand over the children, so Social Services beckoned the waiting police to remove them by force.

A member of the squatters' campaign then approached and told Social Services that my family was not homeless. He informed them that there was another place for us to move into in Ilford.

Before we could be go there, I suffered a series of seizures and was rushed to hospital. I was content there because I knew that Mary and the children were going to be okay in a new property, and I knew I should be out within a few hours.

After a couple of weeks in the new house, there was a knock on the door. It was a well-dressed man in a dark suit, wearing a black hat and carrying an umbrella. He introduced himself as being from the Council and said he wished to talk to the Fleming family. I quite innocently agreed and held the door open to allow him in. As he walked through the open door he rammed me in the stomach with his umbrella, knocking the wind out of me. He then ran through the house to the back door and unlocked it, allowing more men to rush in.

The man in the suit was Barrie Quartermain himself, and his men were waiting at the back of the house to evict us. As this was happening, another squatter who was on the street saw more men approaching the front of the house. He went to let the other squatters know

Hired thugs attempting to evict my family at the Ilford Evictions, London, April 1969

what was happening. In the meantime, over a dozen thugs, including The Seven-Foot Wanderer, who was now attempting to force us out of yet another house, surrounded my family.

The neighbours could hear my children screaming and called the police. Mary was doing her best to calm them, but under these circumstances, it was proving to be very difficult. I was trying to persuade the bailiffs that they needed a court order to evict us and that I wished to see it. The squatters then turned up in numbers and entered the house, prepared to fight off the intruders. The police arrived and questioned the bailiffs, informing them they were acting illegally in the absence of a court order. Quartermain and his evil crew were forced to leave.

It was obvious that we were in constant danger from Quartermain. The police realised that his thugs and the bailiffs were acting illegally and decided that they would post a police presence on our street twenty-four hours a day.

The media, press and the TV 'World in Action' programme asked Mary and me to appear on the show. They treated us very well, until Eamon Andrews interviewed us. He asked me on live TV, "Why are you putting your family through all this?" I was stunned by his question because I was under the impression that his researchers had done their job. It was so obvious he hadn't any background on the circumstances of my family. I stared straight into his eyes and answered, "As long as my wife, my children and I remain together, I will go through anything. You need to ask Barrie Quartermain why *he* is doing this to *my* family." The interview immediately ceased and I got an apology from the producer of the programme.

We were in danger of another eviction attempt. We expected the next one to be more violent and needed to be prepared, as, by this time, the police presence on the street had been removed. The squatters laid booby traps in the back garden, which worried me in case anyone innocent would get hurt by accident.

After a couple of weeks, the bailiffs turned up again in force. We could see that they were carrying shields. Someone shouted an order, and bricks were thrown through the front windows. Several attempts were made to force their way through the front door, but they failed. They erected ladders against the front of the house and tried to gain access through the broken windows.

Mary and the children were taken into the neighbour's house for safety. I remained with the squatters helping to fight off the bailiffs. As the first bailiff reached the top of the ladder and tried to climb in the window, one of the squatters threw petrol over him and produced a box of matches. He had no intention of lighting them, but the bailiff didn't know that. They climbed down in double-quick time and, within minutes, retreated.

The media got involved in broadcasting pictures of the street battle, and so hundreds of people turned up with offers of help and protection for my family. We were really grateful to our fellow squatters who did a great job replacing the broken windows and doing other repair jobs around the house.

One morning about a hundred dockers from the India Docks, South London visited us. In addition, we had a visit from several men from the local boxing club. Among them was Billy Walker, the famous heavyweight boxer. We were overwhelmed to receive such support from so many people. Another surprise visit was from a solicitor and his team who made sure that the Council would not treat my family and me illegally. The media reported on everything that was going on, and at last seemed to be giving their support to us. It caused uproar around the country and further support started to come in from all over.

It was the first time my family felt safe since we had moved into the squat six months earlier. The World in Action programme informed us that Barrie Quartermain had offered to donate money to the 'Fleming Family' because he believed they were genuinely homeless.

Mary sent word back via the World in Action presenter to tell him to keep his blood money.

Here is an excerpt from one of the newspapers from that time. I cannot remember which one.

Redbridge Council was sufficiently 'impressed' to hire the same thugs to deal with its own 'squatter problem'. The men, some of whom sported National Front badges, were supplied by a firm of private bailiffs run by Barry Quartermain who the Sunday Times described as a man who 'tears a London telephone directory into halves and then into quarters as he lectures you about the toughness of his henchmen'. He was later to serve a three-year jail sentence for offences committed in pursuit of his 'business'.

The local council was starting to get embarrassed about the publicity around the Fleming family and offered us temporary accommodation in a ground floor, two-bedroom flat, for a reasonable rent. They agreed to put us on their housing waiting list, and that we would be at the top. This was all great news. I never expected to jump the housing queue, and was very happy that in the meantime my family could live legally in a suitable flat. Mary and I could now settle down with our children without fear of being evicted. Perhaps now I could get off my arse and find a job.

The labour exchange was aware that my epilepsy was a barrier to my normal work options, so they suggested that I go on a one-year course for a diploma in clerical book-keeping and accounts at a residential college in Exeter. I could go home every weekend to see my family and they would pay travel expenses. Mary encouraged me to take the offer. She was fed up with me taking jobs on sites and ending up losing them because of my seizures. I agreed, and was told the college would help me towards securing employment once the course was complete. There were many employers who would take on office employees with epilepsy. The college in Exeter was close to the train station and I was given my own room. I have to say the facilities were perfect.

Exeter is a very military area, and I was surprised to see several British army veterans staying at the college, completing various courses. Many of them had been injured in Northern Ireland and were at the college as a result of their medical conditions.

During the troubles in Northern Ireland and the IRA's campaign in the mainland, being Irish had its disadvantages. Mary and I had learned to keep our mouths shut in the company of English people. It wasn't very pleasant around that time with the mainland bombings. I can't count how many times Mary came home from shopping in tears after being verbally abused and, on one occasion, even refused service in a shop because she was Irish. My children were bullied at school and made to feel unwelcome. There was a couple of times I stayed at home rather than go out to work, just to avoid some English people who were confrontational.

At the college, there was hostility from a couple of the Northern Ireland veterans. Others I found to be helpful. There was one student from Belfast who hung out with the hostile veterans, and made it very clear to me that he was an Orangeman and proud of it. I managed not to be drawn in, and got on with my studies. The course was important to me, and I wanted to ensure I passed every exam to enable me to find permanent employment at the end of the twelve months. But these hostilities were making me feel very uncomfortable and had a negative effect on my studies. The sad thing about it was that there were so many very nice people at the college too.

After eight months, I sat for several exams with good passes and earned my diploma certificate for maths, bookkeeping and accounts.

I went to the pub not far from the college with some of my friends to celebrate my achievement and the guy from Belfast and his veteran mates hassled me. At no time had I ever mentioned to anyone at the college that I too was an army veteran. I didn't see the point. They left the pub around 10.30pm and I stayed on, as I didn't want to leave with them. I had one more pint of ale and left half an hour later.

As I walked out the door the Belfast guy was standing there waiting for me with a broken pint glass in his hand. He made a swipe towards my face with the glass and I managed to duck in time. I could see a car with the doors open outside the pub with its engine running.

Three men grabbed me and pulled me towards the car and tried to get me into it. I knew that I had to make sure these guys never got me into that car because I really believed that they would kill me and dump me somewhere. The Belfast Orangeman had made it very clear to me several times over the months that he would 'sort me out'.

I managed to struggle free from their grasp and made a run across the road towards a golf course. It was dark and impossible to see three feet in front of me, but I carried on running. They were chasing me shouting, "You fucking IRA bastard." I got to a slope and at the bottom of it I thought I saw a road and ran towards it, only to find that there was a big drop into a lake. I turned around and they were in front of me, so I stood my ground. I thought to myself that, whatever happens, I was not going to take this lying down, so I punched and kicked at them until I was forced backwards and fell into the lake. I landed face down into the water and went straight into a seizure. The three guys ran off, leaving me to drown. I wasn't aware that I was drowning because of the seizure. The next thing I remember was the police pulling me out of the water and putting me into an ambulance. They told me I had been drowning when they arrived and that what kept me afloat was my body movement whilst in the seizure.

I was told that the landlord of the pub had called the police, and when the three guys heard the police siren they took off. My foot was very painful and badly cut open because I must have stood on broken glass.

I never told the police who chased me, and after many hours in the hospital I discharged myself. I made my way back to the college with the help of a walking stick, and packed to get ready for the train home the following day.

I had been looking forward to doing an advanced exam, but this could not now happen if I valued my life. I needed to leave as quickly as possible.

I contacted Mary telling her that I would be arriving at Paddington Station around 2pm and would need assistance from there. My foot was killing me during the whole journey and she was waiting with a taxi to take me home. The next morning, I went into another seizure and Mary was worried because I was sweating and had a high temperature. At her request, my GP came out and found that my foot was infected. He treated me with antibiotics and dressed it. I still have nightmares about that college and what might have been had I not managed to escape from those guys that night. The officials there never knew any of this and I chose to leave it like that because I felt very grateful to them and to my teacher who taught me so much.

It was great to be settled back home with Mary and the children, but now it was very important that I go out and find work. The Labour Exchange offered me several office jobs, but the salary was poor, and certainly not enough to feed a family. I applied for a job as a security guard in the West End of London and ended up doing security on exhibitions there. After a couple of months, I was made supervisor and sent to work at the Motor Show. Security was very strict due to the IRA bombings. I was trained up on a bomb detector called the PO3.

On the third day of the exhibition, a couple walked in carrying a suitcase each. I asked them to put their suitcases on the table to enable me to search and apply the detector. As soon as the man heard my Dublin accent, he told me that he also was from Dublin and he and his wife had only just arrived in London. I thought it strange that they came straight to the Motor Show from the airport. He explained that they thought the exhibition would close early and they didn't want to miss it. I gave them the all clear after the search and wished them an enjoyable time at the exhibition.

Two days later, the Dublin man arrived again, this time without his wife, carrying a zipped holdall and attempted to walk through without being searched. I called out to him to have his bag checked and he waved at me shouting, "It's OK Dub, it's me." I demanded he come to the desk for clearance. Something didn't feel right. Once more I insisted that he must come back to be checked in. He made his way over and dropped his bag on the bench. As I was about to unzip it, I looked up and saw him running off.

By now I had my hand inside the bag and was dreading the worst. I called one of the other security lads to bring the detector and test it, bearing in mind my hand was still inside. The detector registered a very high explosive presence and the bomb squad was alerted. The building was evacuated, leaving my security boss, who was an ex-army officer, and myself in the building. I was instructed not to withdraw my hand from the bag until the bomb squad arrived.

That was the longest seven minutes of my life.

The sweat was running down my forehead and I was shaking with fear. As soon as they arrived, the first thing one brave man did was to take my wrist and slowly remove my hand from the inside of the bag. I was then told to leave the building with my security boss and go to a safe area.

Explosives and bomb parts were found in the bag, and it was believed that they had been brought into the exhibition to be assembled inside. A search with sniffer dogs was carried out of the whole building and later on in the evening the all clear was given. I was taken to an office to give the police a statement and a description of the man.

I never heard anything about it after that. I was just glad that we were all safe. The next day, we were back to normal and I continued to search every person who entered the exhibition. One of the exhibitors approached me and handed me an envelope. He thanked me for saving his life. There was £100 in the envelope. We were never allowed to accept gifts from the exhibitors, so I handed it over to my boss. He told me to keep it and take the security staff out for a drink when the exhibition was over.

On one of my days off, I had to drive Mary to Hammersmith Hospital where her sister's husband, Robert, was having one of his kidneys removed. The journey was a complete nightmare, winding through the City towards Westminster and then into the West End. We were stopped twice. There were checkpoints all over, especially in the City of London. Every car was checked. It was 1981, and, with the constant threat IRA attacks, security was very tight everywhere.

We eventually got to the Hammersmith Hospital, and sat with Mary's sister Alice until Robert had his surgery. Afterwards, Mary decided to go to her sister's house and stay with her for a couple of days to help support her during this stressful time.

I set off to drive home alone. I struggled to find my way through London and, when I reached the City, I was stopped at a police roadblock and told to divert right, when I wanted to go straight on. My head was thumping and I was getting very stressed and, a few twists and turns later, found myself back at the same roadblock. One of the policemen signalled me to turn right again and I was back to where I got lost after the first right turn. I pulled in and wrapped both my hands around my head trying to control a growing migraine. I took a few minutes rest but ended up driving towards the same police checkpoint for the third time.

I just couldn't face these same policemen again, so I took a right turn just before the checkpoint and, as I turned, I could see one of the policemen pointing towards me. My headache was getting worse and I was getting more stressed as I drove through side roads. I could see I was getting no closer to home. If only they would have let me drive straight through, I would easily have found my way. I took a turn back on to a main road and, right in front of me, I could see yet another checkpoint. I swore and screamed as I approached it.

Out of nowhere, my car was surrounded and I could hear the siren of a police car approaching me from behind, blocking my car. A policemen opened my door and I haven't a clue what he was shouting, but he looked very angry. I turned my engine off, took the keys from the ignition and stepped out of the car.

Right now, my head was almost exploding and I didn't care what they were going to do with me. I was pinned against my car by two of them who kept asking me questions. I couldn't understand them, and can't remember what I said, but I do remember throwing my car keys at them and shouting, "There's the fucking key, keep the fucking car." Then I attempted to walk away and they followed me down a sidestreet. They must have thought I was a real nutcase.

They moved in on me after several yards and pinned me to the wall, asking question after question. They searched me and found my wallet with all my details inside. One of the other policemen drove my car to where I was being questioned. They kept telling me to calm down and explain why I was in such a state. I explained that I suffered from migraine and I just wanted to get home, but that they prevented me from driving route that I knew. After some minutes, they explained to me why they were a bit rough with me: my Dublin Irish accent. Having checked me out, they returned my car keys and told me to follow their police car until I was satisfied I knew the rest of the way home.

They led me as far as Stratford, and I was able to signal to them that I now knew where I was, so they let me get on my way. It was only after I got home that I realised that seeing my car turn up four times at their checkpoint was enough reason for them to be concerned. But, I never drove into London after that day. Whenever I needed to travel into the city, I used public transport.

Ever since Mary and I were involved in the squatting,

several of the lads who helped us kept in touch and often visited. It was good that we had some friends from the squat who kept in touch.

I came home late one night from my security work, and found Mary in tears and stressed out. She told me that one of the squatters, along with two of his friends, a young couple, visited her. She said they were lovely people and were a great help with the children. When they were leaving, they asked Mary if they could leave their briefcase and pick it up at a later date. After they'd left, she noticed the briefcase was wide open, and, out of curiosity, looked inside. It contained a handgun and hundreds of dollars.

I checked out the handgun, and the magazine was empty. I cleared the breach to ensure it was safe. Both Mary and I were in a panic. This is all I needed – a handgun in my flat for the police to find and link me to the IRA. The next day we contacted the 'friend' from the squat and he told us that the pair he had brought to our flat were members of the Angry Brigade, a left-wing organisation that sent letter bombs to politicians.

Our 'friend' removed the briefcase and said that he would get rid of it. We have no idea what he did with it and didn't care as long as it was never connected to our family. I made a point of cleaning any of our prints from the handgun and the briefcase. He later told me that his two friends left the briefcase open knowing we would find the contents. They thought that, because we were once squatters, we wouldn't mind looking after the case. They thought our flat could be a safe house. I told our squatter 'friend' to tell his two friends never to set foot in our home again and put our family in danger.

twenty one

SECURITY AND REDRESS

For the next few years, I remained with the same security company and got promoted to Deputy Controller. I was earning a decent wage and our children were getting a good education. Our fourth child was born in March 1971, and we named him Brian.

The security company had a contract with the British Film Institute in the West End of London. I was supervising their security, and after several months, they approached me asking if I would work for them full time. I agreed, and took over their security at various buildings across the West End of London. I never told them about my epilepsy, as I felt that I had it under control. Most seizures happened at night, especially in my sleep, so I managed to hide it from them for a couple of years.

While on patrol at one of their buildings off Dean Street, I spotted smoke and called the fire brigade. In the meantime, I managed to evacuate the building and I could see that the fire had started at the bottom of a staircase. In my wisdom, I thought that I could get in under control and went into the building with a fire extinguisher.

Unfortunately, there was far too much smoke and I was overcome by it. I managed to drag myself outside just as the fire engines arrived. They gave me oxygen as I had taken a lot of smoke into my lungs. They put out the fire very quickly and very little damage was done.

I had two seizures while the fireman was treating me. When I woke up, they were talking about getting an ambulance. I got to my feet and told them that I didn't need an ambulance and that I would be okay. My secret was now out in the open and I was terrified they would sack me.

My boss and the personnel department asked to see me the following day to discuss the incident and my future. I was expecting the worst, and the first thing they told me was not to worry about my job. As far as they were concerned, they wanted me to remain in their employment, except I had to agree that everyone within the British Film Institute would be made aware of my medical condition. I wasn't too happy at the thought of all the staff knowing that I had epilepsy, but I was happy to still have a job. Under the Health and Safety Act, my employer couldn't keep me on without putting my medical record on file.

After about a year I got fed up being monitored by the staff, who I know meant well, but it was like they were waiting for me to have a seizure and were far too protective of me. I felt it was time to move on and gave my notice in November 1979. During the following nine weeks I was unemployed, I did some private building work for cash in hand. Work like this was easy to find. I then got a job as security man for a local council, doing shift work.

This suited me perfectly because I was able to hide my epilepsy, especially alone on night duty. I eventually managed to get a mortgage and we bought our first house in Ilford.

In 1990, I applied for a job as a Council inspector that involved checking on contractors' workmanship, and my application was successful. I remained with the local council until my retirement in 1998.

Shortly after I retired, I became unwell and had a minor heart attack. During my time in hospital they discovered that I had leukaemia and I went through many tests to find out the particular type. It turned out that mine was the chronic one. Thankfully, I was told that it was the best type of leukaemia because, although it is not curable, it can be treated and monitored. As long as I took care of myself and avoided catching any chest infections, which could kill me if neglected, I would be fine.

The consultant who diagnosed my leukaemia told me that my life expectancy would be between five to eight years and if I took good care of myself, I could stretch it to ten. That was eighteen years ago, so what do they know, eh?

In 1998 the Irish Gardaí contacted me. They asked me to travel to Dublin to make a statement about what happened to me in the two industrial schools in Ireland. I was 54 years of age and this felt like my demons were catching up on me.

It had emerged that these schools kept punishment books, and the Brothers documented details of every punishment on the boys. The schools were being investigated by the Gardaí regarding sexual abuse, and they were collecting statements from ex-pupils. I could have ignored the Gardaí's request and continued to bury these memories, but it occurred to me that this might be a way to make contact with Ginger, hoping he too would be contacted to attend Gardaí interviews. He was such a great friend I really wanted to see him again.

In Dublin I made my statement to two Gardaí from Cork city. I told them about the beatings I endured at the schools, but I didn't mention the rape. I know I should have told them everything, but I'm a married man with four grown up kids. I had told Mary about the beatings but not about the sexual abuse. Neither did any of my family know about it.

I consulted a solicitor in Dublin who agreed to take on my case, along with many other victims. He insisted that I have counselling before my court appearance. The counselling was a breath of fresh air and, after six sessions, I opened up. Feeling much more courageous, on the evening after my sixth session, I confided in Mary about the sexual abuse. We both cried for ages and I felt so relieved. My counsellor insisted that I write a new statement for the Gardaí detailing the sexual abuse.

I wrote a thirty-page statement outlining everything and explaining why I failed to mention the abuse in my first statement. My counselling went on for four years before I finally felt that I had completely thrown my demons at the doors of the Irish Government and the Church. I asked the Gardaí and the solicitors who represented the survivors if Ginger had been in touch with the authorities, but he hadn't.

During that time I met Danny, who had been in the school with me. He had also been sexually abused. He had made his statement a year before me, and both of our accounts shared the same details about the outhouse where we were taken to be abused. All the victims who made statements were given the choice of taking their case to court or to go before the Redress Board. Going to court would take many years. The Redress Board could deal with it in a year.

The Gardaí told me that Brother Peter was in the USA and had become a priest. He refused to travel back to Ireland to fight his defence, and conceded his guilt. He was well protected by the Church and there was little the Gardaí could do.

In 2002, the day I appeared before the Redress Board in Dublin, was one I can never forget. They made me go through every detail of my abuse. I felt they were putting me through it all again. I collapsed half way through the hearing and had to take a long break. The verdict was that I should be awarded compensation.

I learned that my friend Danny had died a week before his hearing. I attended his funeral.

In all my fifty years living in the UK, I never dwelled on my experience in the Congo. It was like I put it all to the back of my mind. I suppose that had something to do with my anger with the army for discharging me.

In 2012 I was surfing the Internet, and came across a site on the Irish military and decided to add a comment. I told how my family and I were evicted in 1969 in London and explained our belongings were destroyed, including my Congo medal. To my amazement, I received a reply telling me to meet a Kieron Ryan at Liverpool Street station, and that he would replace my medal.

I met Kieron and, as well as replacing the medal, he

introduced me to the Veterans' Association in London. A new chapter in my life opened up, better than I could ever have expected. I joined the Veterans' Association, and now attend three United Nations parades every year, meeting other veterans who also served in the Congo.

It was around this time that I decided to go through the notes I wrote during the seventies and eighties about my experiences in the Congo. I was accepted as a member of a closed Facebook group called 'Irish UN in the Congo.' After some months I shared some of my notes on the page and shortly after that several veterans in Ireland remembered me as having served at the same time as them, in 1961.

I travelled to Athlone, Ireland, in October 2017 for a large parade on the square to show solidarity with veterans who had fought a battle in Jadotville in 1961. It was amazing meeting up with the men I had served with 55 years ago. We were all so young back then, and here we were in our seventies. One veteran I was anxious to meet with, face to face, was Muiris de Barra. He and another unnamed soldier carried me out of a building whilst it was under attack. I was semi-conscious and couldn't stand without falling, so they had to carry me to safety under heavy ground fire. Meeting up with Muiris was the best part of my visit to Athlone, and we now get in touch most days.

I made many friends during these more recent years and still attend the London parades. Marching through Whitehall, London in my uniform is a big thing for me, and meeting many United Nations soldiers from various other countries is a real plus. My photo album is very full and I love going through it and sharing them with my Congo veteran friends in Ireland.

The poor vision in my left eye and the periodic bouts of pain continued for many years until one day, when I was at an optician for a routine test, I was told to get to the hospital as soon as I could to have my eye checked. I went to Moorfields eye hospital and, after x-rays and tests, they informed me that there was a lump the size of a golf-ball behind my left eye. It had been dormant for many years, and I would have to lose that eye. It wasn't a pleasant experience having my eye and the cancer lump removed. Having Leukaemia created complications. The risk of an infection after the surgery would give me less than a 20% chance of survival. The surgeon who gave me the figure may have been trying to scare me into never ignoring a chest infection, but it was a tough statistic to deal with.

I can't help thinking that the injury to my eye during my tour of the Congo had something to do with the eventual removal of my eye.

I was given a UN medal in 1961, then in 2012 received a second medal from the Irish Defence, referring to my service in the Congo. The Defence Force confirmed I was entitled to the medal, which was awarded by Norway to UN soldiers who served before 1988. I was told I had to pay the postage cost to receive the medal, as I was living in London!

In 1996 I met a UN veteran in London who told me that I missed out on receiving the Nobel Peace Prize medal and advised me to contact my barracks in Dublin requesting confirmation. I was entitled to the medal because I served with the UN during the Civil War in the Congo.

In 1988 I was awarded the Nobel Peace medal and received it by post in 2015. Fellow UN veterans in the UK were annoyed that it was not presented to me on parade, and contacted the Irish embassy in London asking the Irish ambassador to attend the UN International Day parade in London. He agreed, and Ambassador Daniel Mulhall presented the medal to me at a reception later that year. I was so proud, even after fifty years, to feel acknowledged as a soldier – a great day for me, and for my family, who were also present.

I came back to Dublin for my brother Jimmy's funeral. During the ceremony in the church we were kneeling with our heads bowed and there was complete silence. I was feeling very emotional, made more so by the side effects of my chemo tablets. My emotions got the better of me and I started to shed a few tears.

Suddenly, with the lubrication of the tears, my false eye slipped out onto the ground in front of me.

It started to roll towards the altar on the wooden floor. The sound was like a coin rolling. All heads lifted, wondering what it was. It rolled right up to the altar and rested at the feet of the priest who had just stepped down from the altar. I'm sure he got a bit of a fright when he saw an eye looking up at him from the wooden floor. God knows what went through his mind. I was so embarrassed, but knew I had to retrieve it quickly before he stepped on it or kicked it. I slipped out from my seat and walked up to the altar, feeling a bit flustered and whispered softly into his ear, "Excuse me, Father. Is there anywhere at the rear I can put my eye back in?" He gulped and I could see his throat pushing in and out. I think he was in shock.

I picked up my false eye, followed his directions and made my way to the rear of the altar, holding my head down in front of the silent crowd. Fortunately, I was able to put it back in and made my way back to my seat.

After the ceremony, I was able to explain to my family and friends what happened and we all had a great laugh about my unfortunate incident.

I like to think that at that very moment, my beloved big brother Jimmy Fleming was looking down on me and was laughing. Rest in peace Jimmy. I never pass a day without thinking of you. I love you. Respect.

Mary and I have four grown up children and three grandchildren, and we are still living in London, growing old gracefully. My twin sister Margaret and brother John are living in Dublin and I get to see them as often as I can.

Medal being presented to Christy by Ambassador Daniel Mulhall, 2015

Noel O'Neill, Gregory Leech & Christy Fleming meet up in Athlone after 55 years, 2017

Writing this book has shown me the importance of having a strong mind and willpower. It has also showed me how important it is to have someone to support you on life's journey.

I always knew that I had my mam's support. My need to see her brought me through the most painful chapters of my life. I always held her love and kindness in my heart and it will always be there. Mam passed away, at the age of ninety, in 2004 from bowel cancer, and it was a terrible blow to the family. I wanted to write my story for many years but held back while she was still alive, because I would never want her to know what happened to me in those schools. Her faith was her life, and I would never wish that to have been taken from her.

Like me, Mam and her two sisters spent part of their childhood in a residential home run by the nuns. Her three brothers emigrated to the UK and ended up in the British army. Thankfully all three survived the Second World War.

During my time in the residential schools in the fifties, my mother continued to fight the authorities to have me returned home. She knew what these residential homes were like from her own childhood experience. The love I had for my mam was unconditional. I adored her and her love made up for the absence of my father.

At one of the most dangerous periods of my life, I knew that I had the support of my fellow comrades and they were always there to cover my back. This was the first time in my life that I felt I could completely trust somebody outside of my family. Again, they will always be in my thoughts and memories, especially many of the army comrades who never came home.

To be able to write this book I needed the skills of both reading and writing. I was not taught by the people who were supposed to educate me, so my brother Jimmy took me on and taught me to read. He opened up a new world to me. For that I will be forever grateful.

What can I say about my wonderful wife Mary? She continued my education in teaching me to write, but she taught me so much more. She brought me love, kindness, patience, tolerance, strength and the belief in myself to never give up. She has been through many a hard time with me throughout our lives. These events brought us even closer together and our love for each other never faltered. We have four wonderful children, Robert, Christopher, Alice and Brian, and the joy and happiness they brought to Mary and me is immeasurable. They added strength to our family unit and gave us more reasons to keep fighting on.

Now in our senior years, we can enjoy being with our grandchildren and our legacy is secure.

The one thing I can't get out of my head is the whereabouts of my friend Ginger, and to this very day I still wonder what happened to him. Maybe this book will find him?

Marching in UN London parade, 2014